Praise for *The Little B*

"*The Little Book of Being* offers new and experienced meditators reliable guidance on the practice of natural awareness, as well as classical mindfulness. Helpful, accessible, and humorous, it makes meditation an inviting adventure while also setting realistic expectations."

GUY ARMSTRONG
author of *Emptiness: A Practical Guide for Meditators*;
guiding teacher, Insight Meditation Society

"Without ever becoming precious or dogmatic, Diana Winston shows how natural, or non-dual, awareness emerges within the continuum of mindfulness practice and is an antidote to the trap of excessive striving. The book is a testament to her years of experience and is a treasure trove of elegant, accessible meditations. Highly recommended for anyone who wants to free their heart and mind."

CHRISTOPHER GERMER, PHD
author of *The Mindful Path to Self-Compassion*;
co-developer of the *Mindful Self-Compassion* program

"In a clear and encouraging voice, Diana Winston points out how the shift from noting *what is happening* to the more spacious awareness *that it is happening* relaxes the mind and body into a state of okay-ness, bringing natural compassion and deep well-being."

SYLVIA BOORSTEIN, PHD
author of *Happiness Is an Inside Job*

"Diana Winston lives and breathes the clean, clear air of mindful awareness and brings a great deal of experience and skill to the table. The practical, accessible, and doable tools and techniques, meditational tips and pointers, and plain ol' wisdom here have helped me discover, recognize, and recover who and what I am—and what we all genuinely are at the level of our very best selves. I believe this will certainly help you, too, release the buoyant little buddha within and live the miraculous life you want and need."

LAMA SURYA DAS
author of *Awakening the Buddha Within: Eight Steps to Enlightenment*;
founder of the Dzogchen Center and Dzogchen Retreats

"Diana Winston's wonderful new book, *The Little Book of Being*, combines the authority of her long and deep practice with her engaging conversational voice—for everyone from beginners to long-time meditators."

SUSAN KAISER GREENLAND
author of *Mindful Games* and *The Mindful Child*

"A rare combination of deep, clear, and accessible wisdom, *The Little Book of Being* is a gem filled with fantastic reflections, practices, and teachings that will nourish new and experienced meditators alike. Written with an engaging freshness, this book reminds us of what we know, love, and regularly forget—the natural awareness that is our very essence."

TARA BRACH, PHD
author of *Radical Acceptance* and *True Refuge*

"*The Little Book of Being* is a lovely, simple, wise, and helpful book. It is filled with down-to-earth practical wisdom, wonderful tools to free the heart, and a perspective of self-kindness that we all need."

JACK KORNFIELD
author of *A Path with Heart*

"*The Little Book of Being* is more than little, and more than about simply being. Diana Winston offers us a big idea about . . . a state of mind we may sometimes call presence—or a 'natural awareness,' in her terms—that research suggests boosts our immunity, reduces inflammation, and can even slow the aging process. Even more, her wise and accessible teachings offer us practical tools for becoming more fully aware and cultivating the clarity and tranquility that arise when the mind accesses this open, receptive state. Take in these powerful ideas and bring more well-being, equanimity, and connection into your life!"

DANIEL J. SIEGEL, MD
clinical professor and founding co-director,
UCLA Mindful Awareness Research Center;
executive director, Mindsight Institute; author of
Aware: The Science and Practice of Presence

"Crafted with kindness, *The Little Book of Being* offers a wonderful invitation to the realm of natural awareness. Weaving clear, concise instruction with encouragement and personal anecdotes, Diana Winston leads us in the direction of a meditation practice free from judgment and striving. Through exercises that point toward short glimpses of natural awareness, we can learn to experience relief from the patterns of our habitual mind."

SHARON SALZBERG
author of *Real Happiness* and *Real Love*

"Breaking new ground, this wise and elegant book, *The Little Book of Being*, is a wonderful guide to the important next stage of mindfulness practice: natural awareness. These down-to-earth essays and short glimpse practices are wisdom bites that are just the right size to enjoy a delicious taste of natural awareness whenever you like. Highly recommended!"

LOCH KELLY, MDIV, LCSW
author of *Shift into Freedom*

THE
LITTLE
BOOK OF
BEING

Also by Diana Winston

Fully Present: The Science, Art, and Practice of Mindfulness
(with Susan L. Smalley, PhD)

Wide Awake: A Buddhist Guide for Teens

THE
LITTLE
BOOK OF
BEING

PRACTICES AND GUIDANCE FOR UNCOVERING
YOUR NATURAL AWARENESS

WITHDRAWN

DIANA WINSTON

BOULDER, COLORADO

Sounds True
Boulder, CO 80306

Published 2019

Book design by Beth Skelley

Printed in Canada

Library of Congress Cataloging-in-Publication Data

Names: Winston, Diana, author.
Title: The little book of being : practices and guidance for uncovering your
    natural awareness / Diana Winston.
Description: Boulder, CO : Sounds True, 2019. | Includes bibliographical
    references.
Identifiers: LCCN 2018030606 (print) | LCCN 2018033671 (ebook) |
    ISBN 9781683643340 (ebook) | ISBN 9781683642176 (pbk.)
Subjects: LCSH: Mindfulness (Psychology). | Awareness. | Meditation.
Classification: LCC BF637.M56 (ebook) | LCC BF637.M56 W56 2019 (print) |
    DDC 158.1—dc23
LC record available at https://lccn.loc.gov/2018030606

10 9 8 7 6 5 4 3 2 1

For Mira, the one and only

CONTENTS

INTRODUCTION

When I was fourteen years old, I spent a summer by the beach as a mother's helper. It was exhausting work, chasing around after a two-year-old and entertaining a six-year-old and keeping the two of them from clobbering each other. I was up to the task, but I didn't often get a lot of downtime.

I remember one night escaping into the field in front of the beach cottage, lying down on a blanket, and looking up at the vast, star-strewn night sky. I let myself fully relax. Without any forewarning, I started to experience a combination of awe and love. In a wave that came over me, I had a sense of being both fully inside my body and as spacious as the sky.

I didn't quite know what to make of this startling experience. I felt love, basically—pure, unconditional love. My mind and body seemed expansive, bright, joyful, and serene—all at the same time. "Wow," I said to myself. "I think I love everyone and everything."

So I tested myself. *Who do I hate?* I came up with my friend's older brother—I'll call him Rex—who used to torment his sister and me whenever I visited. *I definitely hate Rex*, I thought. But in that moment, I couldn't hate him. In that moment, I felt only a sense of love, even for Rex.

I lay there for some time—I couldn't tell you how long—before ultimately getting sleepy and going to bed.

In teaching countless students, I have discovered that many people have had experiences like mine. Frequently, people remember a time in childhood—often when they were in nature, but not always—when they felt a deep relaxation, peace, connection, love, joy, or ease. Or they talk about flow-like states of absorption spontaneously arising as they are participating in sports, creative activities, or intimacy with another person. My assumption when I hear these stories is that the ability to connect with a sense of just being is part of what it means to be human. This quality of being is available to us at any time and has always been available; it just tends to get obscured. We need some specific training to stabilize and deepen our ability to uncover this sense of being, and that is what this book is about.

In my early twenties, when traveling around India and Thailand, I stumbled across Vipassana meditation, a type of Buddhist meditation that offered a path to conceivably make permanent the expansive love I'd felt in the field as a teenager.

Vipassana meditation—sometimes called insight meditation, as it is a pathway to deeper personal insight—has been practiced for more than two thousand years in Southeast Asian Buddhist countries.[1] This meditation practice involves learning to place our attention on present-moment experiences, usually beginning with our breathing, and ultimately learning to be aware on a moment-to-moment basis of all aspects of our experience, such as bodily sensations, thoughts, and emotions. It is a rigorous training in being in the moment. Practicing Vipassana can result in deeply understanding our own psychology and different aspects of reality, such as the impermanent and interconnected nature of life.

While I was a bit skeptical at first, Vipassana soon became my passion. I devoted the next decade to attending silent meditation retreats for several months at a time in monasteries and retreat centers in the United States and Asia. Eventually, I moved to a monastery in Burma (now called Myanmar) to live as a Buddhist nun and practice Vipassana full time.

Ordaining as a Buddhist nun meant shaving my head daily, eating all my meals before noon, wearing salmon-colored nun's robes, and giving away my possessions (although, truthfully, I just put them in storage). I braved snakes and scorpions, unfamiliar food and stomach upset, unbearable heat, and loneliness and isolation, as I missed my family and friends almost constantly.

I spent each day doing sitting and walking meditations in a kind of boot-camp style, diligently applying effort, trying to get my unruly mind to stay solely in the present moment in order to open to insight. When my mind wandered away from my breathing or any other object of awareness, I had to recognize I was lost and then return my attention back to the present moment. I was driven by the vision that if I worked hard enough, I could access deep states of love and awakening. All I had to do was put in enough effort. And throughout that year, I did have many moments of peace, calm, compassion, letting go, equanimity, understanding, and insight. But none of it was ever enough for me.

So I kept trying for more. I persisted, almost obsessively. I limited my sleeping to a meager four hours a night. I tried to meditate for longer and longer hours without moving my posture. I scolded myself every time I realized I wasn't mindful. I knew that if I worked hard enough I would be transformed—or even "enlightened." I needed to have some ultimate and permanent awakening, whatever I thought that was.

After about six months, I exhausted myself, and I suffered a spiritual crisis of sorts. I couldn't meditate; I couldn't think. I was crying all the time. I knew I had to get out of the monastery as quickly as possible.

I went to tell my teacher I was leaving. He was one of the most respected teachers in all of Burma; he was also known as one of the strictest and least warm and fuzzy. Sitting up on his semithrone, behind a fan that half hid his face, he responded, "Well, fine, leave." *That's it*, I thought. *He's not exactly upset I am leaving.* When I stood up to go, his voice boomed, "But if you do, the afflictions of the mind will always overwhelm you."

I returned to my room and cried some more. I had fallen into a despair characterized by deep self-hatred. I felt like an extraordinary failure. The very thing I had set out to do, the one thing I cared about more than anything in my life, I had failed at.

But my teacher's words rang in my mind. My mind sure was filled with afflictions; in fact, at that moment, that was all it was filled with. And if I left, it would certainly continue to be.

So I made a vow that night: I would stay. But I couldn't possibly keep practicing in the same way—struggling, pushing, overefforting. I would try something different, but what?

The first new practice I tried was walking to a nearby lake at dusk each day and crying for a few hours. I imagined my self-hatred being washed away with my tears. I imagined that my perfectionism, my competitiveness, my grief and failure and anxiety were somehow flowing from my body, through my tears, into the vast lake that seemed big enough to hold my pain.

I also discovered some books from Tibetan Buddhist masters in the monastery library. The books explained several things that shifted my practice. First, they said that there is nothing to get and nowhere to go. They explained that awakening is actually inherent to human beings and that love and compassion and freedom are accessible here and now. They also helped me see that deep self-hatred was fueling my practice. I wanted to reach some kind of enlightenment so badly because, truthfully, I didn't want to be me.

In these books I also found a new approach to my Vipassana meditation practice and a range of fresh practices by which to guide myself to more self-compassion. But my biggest recognition was that it was time for me to stop the doing. It was time for me to relax, stop trying so hard, and recognize the natural awareness and goodness already inherent in my being—and in all beings. It was time to simply rest in awareness itself.

A few days after that recognition, when I stood by the lake, the tears began to dry up, and in their wake, a sense of pure self-compassion, awareness, and love overtook me.

The next three months were filled with a sweetness and joy I could never have possibly imagined, as I practiced with and rested my mind in this profound state of well-being, in natural awareness.

In the past twenty years since my time in the monastery, I've had a personal meditation practice that combines both Vipassana and natural awareness practices. Vipassana, or what in this book I call *classical mindfulness meditation*, is my root practice, and it is always there when my mind is distracted, emotionally charged, or lost. But predominately my ongoing practice is to stop the doing and just be. I invite in a natural awareness that is always present (although often obscured) and takes no doing to find. It's as if I tune in to what is already there.

I believe now that classical mindfulness meditation and natural awareness practices go hand in hand. They complement and shape each other.

Classical mindfulness meditation is a fantastic system for stabilizing our minds, cultivating concentration, learning how to work with physical and emotional pain, and developing mental equanimity, or even-mindedness. It can lead to tremendous awakening, as described by experienced students. However, the primary focus of the current mindfulness movement and its teachings—as typified by our Mindful Awareness

Practices (MAPs) classes at the University of California, Los Angeles, and Mindfulness Based Stress Reduction (MBSR), the most well-known secular mindfulness teachings—has been an effort-based mindfulness, an adaptation of the classical mindfulness meditation I learned in the monastery.

The natural awareness view and practices that so changed my life and healed deep wounds inside me are not generally being taught in the secular mindfulness world, except implicitly. So over the years, I have begun to expand my teaching to also offer students a range of natural awareness practices.

There are multiple ways in which to be aware: from the effortful to the effortless, from the narrowly focused to the wide open and spacious, from awareness of objects to objectless awareness of awareness. (Objects are things we are aware of when we meditate, like our breath, sounds, body, and emotions.) These means of being aware fall on a spectrum. Almost all contemporary mindfulness books detail and elaborate the effortful, narrow, and object-based end of the awareness spectrum. Over the years, I have developed many commonsense approaches to exploring and navigating the effortless, spacious, and objectless end of the awareness spectrum, which is often seen as available only to more established or advanced meditators. When I started teaching these practices at the UCLA Mindful Awareness Research Center, I was excited to see how beneficial they were to a wide variety of students.

This book is intended to serve as a guide to that effortless, spacious, and objectless end of the awareness spectrum. It shows that anyone can access natural awareness, and it offers down-to-earth tools for doing so. My hope is to round out, demystify, clarify, and help practitioners understand this seemingly advanced practice.

There are many reasons you might pick up this book: You may have been practicing classical mindfulness meditation for some time and be curious about what other approaches are out there. Maybe you are looking for ways to invigorate your longtime meditation practice, which has become mundane and routine. Or it could be that my story from that time in Burma rings familiar to you; perhaps you too have been working too hard at meditation, or you are caught in judgments and comparisons and can't seem to soften and relax in meditation. Or possibly, as many of my students have experienced, you've been organically exploring natural awareness during meditation all along, and you're looking for a guidebook to clarify the territory you've been discovering.

Or it could be that you're newer to meditation and feel drawn to a spacious, relaxed awareness practice. Or perhaps what I'm describing just feels familiar to you in some way, regardless of your meditation experience. Maybe you have experienced profound mind states in meditation or life and you're looking for practices to help you dive in more deeply.

If you have some classical mindfulness meditation experience, the practices in this book can complement and augment your existing practice. If you're new to classical mindfulness meditation, this book includes chapters that will instruct you in the basics of it so that you will have a springboard from which to jump into natural awareness meditation.

The book is written in short, essay-style chapters meant to be easily digestible and accessible to any reader. I do my best to not make the subject intimidating and to use language that is as commonsensical and approachable as I can come up with.

The first part of the book, "Foundations: Understanding Natural Awareness," provides a basic overview of natural awareness, explaining what it is and why and how you might want to learn and practice with it. The second part, "Techniques: Meditating with Natural Awareness," offers guidance for practicing both classical mindfulness and natural awareness meditations. I begin this part with instructions on classical mindfulness meditation, a helpful starting point, and show you how to shift into natural awareness meditation. Then I offer techniques and guidance for addressing the kinds of issues you may encounter as you practice with both types of meditation. The third part, "Embodiment: Living Natural Awareness," shares tools and guidance for recognizing whispers of natural awareness already present in life and for finding ways to informally practice with natural awareness on a daily basis, so that you can function more fully from this open, aware, luminous state of mind.

Peppered throughout the book are "glimpse practices," short practices that can be done as part of a daily meditation routine or at any point in the day when you wish to access natural awareness. They can be utilized for a few seconds, a few minutes, or longer, as you wish. See "How to Use the Glimpse Practices" below for detailed instructions.

At first natural awareness may seem far away, just a whisper, but then it will begin to grow and expand and permeate aspects of life. Over time, as you continue to dip into natural awareness again and again, you may feel more peace, more connection to yourself. You may find yourself taking life a bit more lightly. You may feel a sense of relaxed "beingness" throughout the day, and when you do get caught in your dramas (as we all do), you may find yourself moving out of them more quickly than you imagined you could.

Once you get the hang of tuning in to it, natural awareness becomes a constant companion—sometimes elusive, but always available when you remember it and seek it out. And with it, you will live with the benefit of the deepest sense of well-being possible: the well-being of coming home to yourself.

HOW TO USE THE GLIMPSE PRACTICES

The glimpse practices throughout the book will help you experience natural awareness. They are practices I have either learned from teachers over the years or developed through my own practice and teaching. Most of the glimpse practices involve specific techniques or mental shifts you can make in order to evoke or experience natural awareness. Others use quotes, analogies, or phrases to evoke the qualities of natural awareness. Glimpse practices can be used during a meditation session or at any point in daily life.

To use a glimpse practice as a part of your meditation, I recommend starting with classical mindfulness meditation to stabilize your mind. Once you have a sense that your mind is calm(ish) and somewhat focused, employ one of the glimpse practices and see what happens. Drop a glimpse practice into your concentrated, meditative mind, give it a little time, and notice the effect.

Many things can occur. You might find that you try it and think, *So what? Nah, that didn't do anything.* In that case, try another one. Try five. See which one, if any, you respond to.

Or you might try a glimpse practice and get a vague sense that you're entering the territory of natural awareness, but not in a full way. Rest in that recognition. It's nice to be close.

In either of these two cases, it might feel right to return to more classical mindfulness meditation or to use any of the tools described throughout this book to help you where you're stuck. Or you might just stop for now and try again later.

Another day you might try a glimpse practice and feel an immediate connection to an experience of natural awareness and to the luminous nature of your mind. This connection might last a few seconds, a few minutes, or much longer. If you can, abide or rest in it. Then as it fades away, depending on how much time you have, you could try another glimpse practice.

To use the glimpse practices in the midst of daily life, give one a try whenever you remember or feel moved to do so. At any moment you can remind yourself of a glimpse practice and can explore what happens when you use it on the spot. There's no need to prepare your mind in any particular way, as you would when using glimpse practices in meditation. Simply pick a practice, try it, and observe what happens. Taking a few breaths in advance could be useful, but it is not necessary.

Sometimes the glimpse practices grow a bit stale, and you have to rotate through them. Many of them will be completely useless to you, or you'll have no idea what they mean. Others will feel profoundly helpful. And their usefulness may change over time. You might find one difficult or confusing now but come to appreciate it later on.

I also encourage you to make up your own glimpse practices. Once you get a sense of what you are aiming for, you will find your own creative entrée into natural awareness.

As you can see, there are no rules here—just experimentation in the spirit of more and more wakefulness. So have fun with the process, and please don't beat yourself up when it feels like it's not "working." The point isn't to be a natural awareness master, successful at evoking natural awareness in any and every moment (although if that happens, please let me know). The point is to gain the ability to work with your mind in a skillful way to cultivate more and more freedom.

PART I

FOUNDATIONS

UNDERSTANDING NATURAL AWARENESS

1 ❧ WHAT IS NATURAL AWARENESS?

Awareness is a capacity of the human mind. Awareness is the ability to directly know and to perceive, sense, feel, or be cognizant of experience.[1] We might think of awareness simply as the state of being conscious of something.

Every living being is aware. We usually don't think much about awareness, but in order to function, humans have to be aware. Not only do humans have the capacity to be aware, but they also have the ability to be aware of awareness, or aware that they are aware. Let's try this simple experiment:

 Right now, put down the book and don't be aware. In the next minute, please stop being aware. I mean it. Ready, go . . .

Are you back? Could you *not* be aware? No, you couldn't. This capacity to be aware is a function of the human mind. And in this exercise, you noticed that you were aware and that it's impossible to stop being aware.

However, being aware is not natural awareness. Natural awareness is very hard to explain (and that's why it takes me the next 208 pages!), but here's the synopsis: Natural awareness is a way of knowing and a state of being wherein our focus is on the awareness itself rather than on the things we are aware of. It is generally relaxed, effortless, and spacious.

Natural awareness can subjectively feel very powerful. It can feel like a deep sense of peace, joy, love, contentment, serenity, connection, and much more. It can be evoked through specific practices, and it is a type of meditation in and of itself. It can become a familiar state, accessible in daily life and regularly experienced as you meditate with it over time.

Because natural awareness is hard to define, it is primarily recognized experientially. Let me give you some markers of it. Natural awareness can feel like:

- Your mind is completely aware and undistracted without you doing anything in particular to make yourself aware.

- Your mind is like wide open space, and everything in it is just passing by.

- You are aware but not identified with the part of you that is aware.

- Your mind feels at rest.

- You are noticing that you are noticing, and you are abiding in that awareness.

- Everything just seems to be happening on its own.

- You feel a sense of contentment not connected to external conditions.

- You are simply being—without agenda—and this beingness creates a feeling of timelessness and ease.

You can experience natural awareness in one of these ways or some combination of them. Everyone experiences it in different ways, and how you experience it can vary from day to day.

Maybe one or more of the markers above makes sense to you. If you think you have had a taste of natural awareness or entered the territory of natural awareness, please trust that. Any experiential sense of natural awareness will become a touchstone that you can always return to during your meditation practice or in life.

2 \ WHAT MAKES NATURAL AWARENESS NATURAL?

I call this type of awareness *natural awareness* because this name seems to be the best one to get at its qualities:

It's natural or inherent to all humans. All humans have had experiences during which their mind seems to rest in a place of ease or well-being. In the introduction, I shared my own story of accessing this place as a teenager. Countless students have told me of times that they encountered this territory when they were in nature, playing sports, or viewing art. One student told me that the second she heard a description of natural awareness, she remembered sitting under a tree in the woods on a fall day as a small child, her mind entirely at rest. Another shared that throughout his life, he had encountered a profound sense of ease and immersion while shooting hoops. Another student was reminded of early days in her marriage when she and her partner would sit on the porch listening to old records (yes, this was a while ago). They had no agenda; they just listened and sat and "be'd" together. (Recollecting this memory actually led quite naturally to her opening to natural awareness in that moment.)

Many of us can recall a sense of "just being." Just being isn't natural awareness, but it is evocative of it and in the same territory.

It's natural in that it's always available, if we can find it. The term *natural awareness* invites us to notice or rediscover the awareness that already exists and is available at any moment.

I like the following analogy, which I learned from Loch Kelly, a teacher of "effortless mindfulness": Natural awareness is like a radio station that is always blasting and is always available to us. However, much of the time we are tuned to a different radio station. We tend to tune to station anxiety, station catastrophizing, KPFJudgment, or WNCAnger. So even though natural awareness is part of being human, we need to practice tuning in to it in order for it to become the radio station we listen to most often.

The word *natural* helps evoke it. I also like the term natural awareness because the words themselves seem to evoke a quality of resting, letting go, letting things be—all of which are qualities of the awareness I'm pointing to. It arises when our minds let go. Much of the time we're caught in our drama and what we might call *ordinary mind*. We are holding tight to our opinions, beliefs, desires, and so on. We basically believe our own stories 99 percent of the time. However, we can learn to let go of these stories, and when we do, we find a freedom of mind—a mind that's not clinging to anything. What is here in the wake of clinging, when we really investigate? You'd be right if you guessed a natural awareness.

RECOLLECTION

One of the simplest ways to access natural awareness is through memory. Let yourself remember
a time when you felt awake, connected, peaceful,
expansive—in a state of "beingness." Recall this
time. Don't try too hard; let it come to you in a
simple way.

Perhaps you were in nature, in the midst of
athletic activity, in the creative flow, lying at rest
in bed, with a lover, or laughing uproariously with
your best friend. Can you remember where you
were? What did you see? Hear? Now remember
how you felt at the time. What did your body feel
like? How about your heart? See if you can invite
in a full-bodied experience of the memory. Recall
details: sight, scents, sounds, any other sensory
experience.

Now notice what is happening in the present
moment. See if a sense of beingness is present for
you, just by your imagining a past experience. What
does that beingness feel like? Connectedness, ease,
presence, relaxation? Let yourself rest here.

3 ❧ WHY IS NATURAL AWARENESS SO HARD TO FIND?

If natural awareness is part of what it means to be a human being and is always available, why isn't everyone walking around resting their minds in it? Why do we have just occasional whispers of it, if that? Why does it feel so far away?

There are so many answers to these questions. Some of the ancient teachings tell us that natural awareness is too obvious, too close—as close as our face, some say. It's also so subtle that it is almost impossible to recognize unless it has been pointed out to you. Or else it's too easy to recognize! It's right here, and yet we miss it all the time. Clearly, it's not intuitively easy to first recognize and then sustain or deepen our experience of it, nor is it easy find our way back to it regularly and at will.

Resting our minds in natural awareness also seems to be the opposite of how most people typically live. Most of us are lost in ordinary mind. We are caught in our dramas, lost in habitual reactivity, anxiety, irritation, or sadness. Or we are checked out, operating on automatic pilot, just kind of going through the motions as we sail through life. Either way, we're missing much of our lives. Ordinary mind feels familiar.

Connecting to natural awareness can feel counterintuitive, or it can simply feel unfamiliar to most people. We are used to our habitual states of mind, and so we stay in them most of the time. Those moments when we taste something different, such as in the creative or athletic flow, are like little bleeps that wake us up and point to something wonderful beyond our small self, but that is not our usual mode of being.

Plus we live in a world that seems to be about evoking the opposite of natural awareness. Most people, at least in the globally northern world, tend to be living a life of speed and distraction. Distraction from what? Well, from ourselves. The worlds we inhabit are practically invented to keep us from looking inward. There are television and technology and smart-phones and tablets and 24/7 news cycles and invasive media. Our devices in and of themselves aren't necessarily inherently harmful, but most of us use them to check out of ourselves, rather than check in with ourselves.

Then there's the ever-present to-do list that we can never get to the bottom of. Personally, I have a university mindful-ness center to run, with the endless tasks that entails; I have to get my daughter's permission slip for the beach cleanup filled out by tomorrow; and I have about four hundred emails clut-tering up my inbox. If I listen to and take seriously a voice that says, "You have too much to do," I will never meditate. I am way too busy a person to foster awareness! And when we finally check off everything on our to-do list, there's always the "should" list: I should clean out my files, repair my bicycle, and get my daughter into another one of those classes she doesn't really need.

Put all of this together, add a sprinkling of despair at the state of the world, economic uncertainty, environmental catastrophe, or just making ends meet, and sure enough, you will begin to see that accessing natural awareness is not so easy—at least on your own.

4 ◗ WHAT'S IN IT FOR ME?

Natural awareness is one of many ways of being aware, and awareness is good no matter how you slice it. But there are many other reasons why you might be drawn to a natural awareness practice:

You've already experienced natural awareness. While you are meditating, you might find that, although you are trying to keep your attention on a focus point, like your breath, your mind keeps settling into a more spacious, open awareness. It seems like natural awareness is where your meditation practice wants to take you at the moment.

You've gotten some of the goodies already. Perhaps you are already accessing natural awareness and are experiencing its fruits. For example, maybe you feel more peaceful and calm or have experienced profound feelings of well-being and ease, and those feelings seem to bleed over into your daily life.

You've been working too hard. I have met many students of classical mindfulness meditation over the years (and, I confess, I was one of them) who exert massive amounts of energy to keep their attention focused, who try to be aware of every moment, and who often feel a disturbing tightness and tension in their meditation practice. When they begin to relax into a more natural awareness, the struggle ceases, and they find they can continue to practice with much greater ease and spaciousness. They don't have to try so hard to be aware.

You need something to counteract self-judgment. Practitioners often judge their meditation practice and themselves ruthlessly.

I remember in my early years of practice I told a friend I was a terrible mindfulness practitioner because I could be mindful only about ten times during the day. He gently replied, "Why don't you reframe it? 'How *wonderful*—I am mindful ten times in a day!'" I carried a lot of self-judgment, and the narrative in my head was rife with criticisms like *You're not doing this well enough!* When I began to practice tuning in to natural awareness, I realized there was nothing really to get and that inherently my mind was already aware. The judging inner critic soon went on sabbatical (and now visits only from time to time).

You're looking for freedom from mind chatter. Natural awareness practices are not about working hard to calm our wild mind but about shifting into an already existing place of rest and freedom beneath the chatter. An analogy that's often used is moving from the turbulence of the waves above into the deep stillness of the ocean below. As my dear friend Wim, who passed away many years ago, used to say, "Would you rather have a mind lost in thought or resting in awareness? You decide."

You want to be free of your dramas. Our mind is usually busy defending, worrying, explaining, fighting, and comparing. Natural awareness offers another way for our mind to be—a way that is not lost in these dramas but that has a feel of freedom to it. In experiencing natural awareness, we let go. And when we let go, what is there in the wake of letting go? The goodness of our own mind—the space of a mind free of drama. This is a sacred place. We usually just zip past it—"Phew! I'm no longer caught in my story. I'm not in pain anymore"—and then we move on. But we can learn to rest in this freedom.

You want freedom from ego drama and polarization. It's extraordinary when we can step aside from our usual focus on me, me, me—on our separateness—and open to a sense of something greater than our own small ego dramas. Spending time in natural awareness is an amazing antidote to the self-centeredness and polarization that our world is rife with. The practice of accessing natural awareness could potentially change our ego-driven behavior.

It's lovely. Sometimes when accessing natural awareness we feel a lovely sense of compassion, kindness, interconnection, joy, and radiance. Think how your embodiment of these qualities can impact all whom you meet.

5 ◗ UM, WHAT IS MEDITATION?

I consider meditation to be any practice that cultivates inward investigation. It is as simple as that. The word *meditation* is a giant umbrella term for these practices, and there are many types of practices that fall under it.

You can think of it in the way we think of sports. *Sports* is the general word, and there are dozens of categories of sports: land activities, water activities, ball related, animal oriented, and so on. Within each category there are often countless variations of sports: beach volleyball, land volleyball, pool volleyball, and so on.

There are dozens of categories of meditation, including concentration practices, positive emotions practices, physical meditations, prayer, and healing practices. Within each of these categories are practices that are endlessly creative and generative, and I couldn't even begin to count them, just as new sports are continually being invented. (Have you heard of chess boxing, cheese rolling, or extreme ironing?)

Awareness practices are a particular category of meditation. Awareness practices can teach us how to cultivate awareness and how to recognize, prolong, stabilize, and live from awareness. This book focuses only on awareness practices and not on any other type of meditation. We won't be exploring visualization or walking a labyrinth, prayer, or other contemplative practices, all of which are valuable but outside the scope of this book.

Within the category of awareness practices is classical mindfulness meditation. Because it has gained quite a bit of currency in the West in the past decade, we might think of classical mindfulness meditation as the baseball of meditation—well-known, frequently practiced, and well loved. (Although it's hardly a spectator sport. In fact, I can't think of anything more boring than watching someone do classical mindfulness meditation. But then again, lots of people say that about baseball, too.)

For more about classical mindfulness meditation, please see chapter 6 and chapters 15 through 19.

A Word about the Word *Practice*

I have already used the word *practice* many times, so let me take a moment to clarify the meaning. *Practice* means to actively and deliberately work, generally through repetition, to develop or cultivate something, usually a skill. To become proficient at playing a musical instrument, for example, we practice daily, often for hours. Meditation is no exception; it requires ongoing, regular, daily practice in order for one to develop facility.

Meditators tend to refer to meditating simply as *practicing*; we might say, "I practiced this morning for thirty minutes" or "I didn't practice at all yesterday. I'm a slacker!" An outside observer might be confused. Practice what? For whatever reason, *practice* has become shorthand for "meditating." To confuse things even further, we also call meditations themselves *practices*. "How is your practice going?" is a common question that means, "How is your meditation practice coming along?"

Also confusing is how we can use the word *practice* not just to mean meditation but also to mean a shift of mind you can deliberately make at any moment. An example of this is what I call the *glimpse practices* throughout the book. They are not full-on, extended meditation sessions, but short moments of practicing natural awareness that can be employed in the midst of your daily meditation practice or any time during the day.

ASK YOURSELF . . .

Try this practice at any moment. In meditation you might want to focus your mind before you employ it. In daily life, try it when you feel drawn to.

Turn your attention to whatever is happening in the moment, which we might call "just this." "Just this" could be anything—thoughts, emotions, sensations, sounds, your breath, the visual field, or some combination of these things. Then drop the following question into your mind and see what happens, as if you were dropping a stone into a pond to notice the ripples:

"Is it okay to be aware of just this?"

6 ❧ BUT WHAT ABOUT REGULAR OLD MINDFULNESS PRACTICE?

Perhaps you have been practicing mindfulness meditation for some time, and now you've picked up this book. You may be quite confused. Have you been wasting your time? Have you been practicing an inferior form of meditation and only now are finding the secret, advanced teachings?

No!

Practicing mindfulness meditation may well have been life changing for you. You may have found that your mindfulness meditation practice has given you a way to reduce stress, build attention, regulate emotions, and cultivate states of well-being. These are no small things. But mindfulness is not the full picture of how one can cultivate awareness.

For the sake of this book, I'll call the practice you have been doing *classical mindfulness meditation*. I need to distinguish this familiar way of practicing meditation from natural awareness practices. *Classical mindfulness meditation* is an imperfect term because natural awareness practice is also classical (that is, rooted in its own tradition) and there are forms of classical mindfulness meditation that enter the territory of natural awareness. But hang in here with me, and you'll see why the distinction is useful in our contemporary meditation context. You will also see that many of the general instructions throughout the book apply to both kinds of practices.

Mindfulness 101: The Basics

I define *mindfulness* as paying attention to our present-moment experiences with openness, curiosity, and a willingness to be with what is. It is a deliberate application of attention. Mindfulness itself is experienced and cultivated through practicing classical mindfulness meditation. Classical mindfulness meditation typically involves placing your attention on a main object of awareness, such as your breathing, and when your wily attention wanders away, you gently but firmly bring it back to your main focus. Over time, as your mind gains stability, you learn to expand your attention to other objects of awareness (such as sounds, sensations, emotions, or thoughts).

Additionally, mindfulness is a *quality of attention* that you can bring to any moment and practice daily in an informal way. So once you understand how to be mindful, you can be mindful in the midst of your day just by remembering to be mindful in that moment. Noticing sensations in your body or the feel of your breath in the present moment is one great way to be informally mindful. You can then bring mindfulness into a daily activity like showering or eating. You can be mindful while walking or exercising. People often practice being mindful in a moment of stress or during strong, difficult emotions.

If you are new to the practice of classical mindfulness meditation, chapters 15 through 19 will give you much more detail about it. Many students find it is helpful to begin with classical mindfulness meditation before moving to natural awareness meditation, which is why you'll find that classical mindfulness meditation instructions appear first in this book. Some people do jump right into natural awareness meditation.

7 ◗ THE SPECTRUM OF AWARENESS PRACTICES

Go to a window with a busy, active street scene outside of it—one with lots of cars. Or you can imagine this scenario in your mind's eye.

Look out the window. First, make an effort to focus on one car. Follow it as it enters your view out the window and then exits the other side. Choose a few more cars and observe them in this way.

Next, rather than following one car from one side of the window to the other, notice other cars in the scene, one by one. Focus with some effort, but not as intensely as before. Then let your attention go to whatever grabs it, in no particular order. You might notice a blue sedan, then a plumbing truck, then a minivan. Where is your attention drawn? Watch with curiosity as the vehicles grab your attention.

Finally, look out the window again and take in the whole view in front of you. Instead of focusing on any one vehicle or multiple vehicles one by one, can you notice, really, pretty much everything? Can you even notice aspects of your view that might not be in the foreground—like the road or the sky? You may not notice the scene with a lot of specificity, as you did in the earlier views, but can you observe the whole scene in a spacious, relaxed, seemingly effortless way—and still notice the complexity of the many things happening in front of you? Stay here for a while.

As a bonus, see if you can even notice the part of you that is aware of the scene in front of you, looking through the window at the whole view. Can you become aware that you are aware of looking? This part is tricky. Some students report a dissolving of the viewer or sense that they are both perceiving the scene and part of the scene.

This exercise helps you see the different ways you can be aware: focused, flexible, and natural, in that order. Different types of awareness practices cultivate each of the three types of awareness. When you put them on a continuum, you can see how they relate to one another. In this book I will concentrate primarily on natural awareness practice, but will also include the other types of awareness practices, since, as this continuum shows, they are related to one another. They're just employing different ways of being aware. I call this continuum the *spectrum of awareness practices*.

The Spectrum of Awareness Practices

A spectrum with three types of awareness practices looks like this:

FOCUSED AWARENESS PRACTICE   FLEXIBLE AWARENESS PRACTICE   NATURAL AWARENESS PRACTICE

This is the technical part, so hang in here with me. At one end of the spectrum is what we might call *focused awareness practice*. When we are practicing focused awareness, we're making an effort and focusing narrowly on an object—often our breath. When our attention wanders, we notice it has wandered and then return our attention to our breath (or other object of focus). Focused awareness practice is the classical mindfulness meditation practice most people begin with, and it is useful for training unruly minds. It helps us develop stabilization, concentration, and clarity of mind. As you can imagine, it often takes a lot of effort. Focused awareness practice is like tracking a single car as we look out a window.

Next along the spectrum is what we might call *flexible awareness practice*, which is also taught within classical mindfulness meditation. When we are practicing flexible awareness, our awareness has a wider field, rather than being narrowed to only one central focus (like our breath). Sometimes we flexibly move our attention to investigate other objects of awareness that pull us away from our main focus (such as a sound, a sensation, or an emotion) and then return to our main focus after a while. Sometimes our attention may appear to jump around from object to object, and we rarely return to a main focus. Effort is variable, attention is both broad and narrow, and we still focus on objects. Flexible awareness practice, in our window analogy, is attending to whatever vehicle grabs our attention as we look out the window.

On the far end of the spectrum is *natural awareness practice*, which is not commonly included in classical mindfulness meditation. Natural awareness practice is usually effortless and objectless, emphasizing awareness of awareness. With natural awareness practice, we don't have to try so hard. Our mind tends to rest in a place of ease, and awareness seems to happen on its own. Typically, attention is broad, and it doesn't focus on objects. In our analogy, natural awareness is sitting back and taking in the whole scene simultaneously and without focusing on specific vehicles, even turning our attention to *awareness itself*. Despite not trying to focus, we can effortlessly be aware of the scene.

These three types of awareness practices are not fixed points on the spectrum; there are degrees of each practice, and they blend into one another. There may be other variations along the way, but these three are the main ones. They are different ways that our meditation practice can manifest itself at different times. Sometimes they occur in combination, as if you're doing several things at once.

The most important thing to know is that awareness practices fall on a horizontal spectrum, *not* in a vertical hierarchy or in levels, and are thoroughly related to one another. And they differently emphasize degrees of effort, focus, and objects, as we will talk more about throughout the book.

I often use a single three-step guided meditation practice to teach students about these three individual awareness practices. I teach them in this way, not because one awareness practice is better than another, but because I think it is helpful to have a single set of steps to move our attention from focused awareness (with which meditators are most familiar) to natural awareness (with which meditators are usually least familiar). Flexible awareness practice is a great intermediary step, as it combines elements from each of the other awareness practices at the opposite ends of the spectrum. I've included my three-step guided meditation practice in the appendix, so you can try it yourself.

Sailing, Diving, and More

Here is my favorite analogy to describe the spectrum of awareness practices. It came from a student who has been meditating for some time.

Focused awareness practice is like being a sailor who is trying to keep a sailboat on course. The sailor adjusts the tiller left or right to navigate where the boat is heading. If it goes off course, he moves the tiller accordingly. The sailor has a destination and is working to reach it. He may feel mastery, purpose, and clarity.

Flexible awareness practice is like being a scuba diver. The scuba diver is underwater, eyes wide open, observing the array of fish, coral, and plant life that swim by or float in front of her. She can adjust her depth and amount of oxygen to investigate a particular fish, perhaps; she can also relax in one place and notice what drifts through the sparkling water in her field of vision. Scuba divers often describe a deep sense of peace and awe at the exquisite variety of undersea life.

Natural awareness practice—well, it's sort of like being the water itself.

8 ✴ DID I SAY, "NO HIERARCHY"?

Here is the most important part of understanding the spectrum of awareness practices: there is no hierarchy.

Oftentimes people think that natural awareness practice is better than the other types of awareness practices because it seems kind of cool or special or more advanced and because they find themselves practicing natural awareness after working for a long time in their classical mindfulness practice. Also, a lot of the religious literature, such as texts from some Buddhist schools, seems to point to it as the "highest" or most special way to practice.

In truth, there is no high-class awareness practice lording it over the other types of awareness practices. There are just different ways of practicing with awareness, and they can occur or be used at different times, both in life in general and in meditation specifically. Meditation students explore and utilize different ways of being aware at different times in their practice, based on what they need or what is arising for them; in meditation jargon, employing different practices at different times and circumstances is called *skillful means*. Another definition of *skillful means* is "whatever works." Is your current practice leading to more joy, more emotional regulation, more ease of being, less drama? Then it's the right one to do!

Your practice, like mine, may move through the full spectrum of awareness practices in the course of a session, over many sessions, and over time—even over years. Sometimes one type of practice is called for more than another. Sometimes one type spontaneously arises at one time versus another type. It's helpful to go with whatever type of awareness practice arises in your meditation and pay attention to what feels organic and natural, rather than contriving to make your meditation be a certain way that it's not. In other words, if you find yourself in meditation spontaneously focusing on your breath or, conversely, noticing multiple aspects of your experience simultaneously, then go with it. Over time, we learn to be our own best teacher.

REMINDER PHRASES

Natural awareness can sometimes be evoked with phrases that remind us of our own luminous awareness. It can be helpful to have a stable, concentrated, and somewhat receptive mind before you state the phrase in your mind and notice the impact (as if dropping a pebble into a pond and noticing the ripples), but it is also fine to use a reminder phrase at any moment. Here are a few you can try (attributed, when applicable, to the meditation teachers who taught them to me):

"Rest in the way things are." (Guy Armstrong)

"Mind luminous like the sun."

"Mind of no clinging." (Joseph Goldstein)

"Everything happens on its own."

"Aware of awareness."

"Our mind is like the sky, vast, open, and spacious; thoughts are like clouds floating by."

9 ❧ THE SCIENCE OF NATURAL AWARENESS PRACTICE

Classical mindfulness meditation has been researched significantly in the past thirty years, although more so in the twenty-first century. It's still a young field, with only about four thousand published studies as of this writing. That may sound like a lot, except that if you were to do a search on PubMed, the online medical-journal database of citations and abstracts (maintained by the National Center for Biotechnology Information in the United States), for studies showing that exercise is helpful for people with heart disease, you would find more than sixty thousand studies. Also, many of the mindfulness studies have not been replicated, use small sample sizes, and don't have adequate control groups. In spite of all these limitations, the science of mindfulness has been promising, and the field is growing.

Generally, classical mindfulness meditation has been shown to improve health outcomes for stress-related conditions, reduce pain symptoms, improve emotional regulation, help with anxiety and depression, increase the ability to pay attention, and cultivate states of well-being. The neuroscience research even shows structural brain changes in long-term meditators.

However, when I look for the science connected to natural awareness practice, I notice that most research has focused primarily on classical mindfulness meditation. There has been some research comparing *focused attention meditation* (FAM) to what is called *open monitoring meditation* (OMM). FAM is basically what I refer to as *focused awareness meditation*, making an effort to stay focused on an object, like your breathing. In OMM, the focus of awareness is the monitoring of awareness itself—that is, natural awareness. (That said, when I review the literature, it seems to me there is variety in how scientists describe OMM, and some of the definitions seem to match my definition of flexible awareness more closely than the definition of natural awareness.)

The FAM and OMM research shows that different kinds of meditation are associated with different neural structures and different patterns of EEG activity.[1] Some of the differences include increased theta activity in the brain (a state connected to deep relaxation) in OMM and acquisition of broader attentional scope in OMM, as you could probably imagine would be the case. Both FAM and OMM improve executive attention, as tested through the Attentional Network Task (which tests three different attentional networks), and may be helpful with mood disorders.

There is much more to be done with meditation research in general, and researching natural awareness specifically may reveal that it offers benefits similar to those of classical mindfulness meditation or additional benefits. I look forward to seeing the results down the road.

10 ❧ NATURAL AWARENESS
IN LIGHT OF RELIGION

What I'm calling natural awareness is described in different religious and spiritual traditions in varied ways. You hear it referred to as *Buddha nature, true nature, luminous mind,* and *nondual awareness.* I've had students tell me it's how they experience God. I've heard it described as *the ground of our being, awakened awareness,* and even *the nature of everything.* Many of these descriptions come from Buddhist teachings and Hindu Advaita Vedanta, but you can also find some analogous teachings in most religions, including indigenous ones.

To me, accessing natural awareness is an inherent capacity of the human mind that's not dependent on religion but has been codified within religious traditions. I teach natural awareness practice as a technique. But then, you may wonder, does this make natural awareness less sacred? Since natural awareness is experiential, I believe it is as sacred as each individual personally experiences and makes sense of it. For some it is deeply sacred; others may have a scientific interpretation of their experience.

I always love the analogy of many blind men describing an elephant. One holds the trunk and says an elephant is tube-like. Another feels its tail and thinks the elephant is like a string. A third touches its backside and assumes an elephant is a giant, boulder-like creature. Which is true? Well, each is the individual blind man's experience. And all are true—partial, but true.

You may notice that I am pointing you toward a territory, even mapping out a bit of what it's like when you enter it, but I am definitely not telling you what you are going to experience when you're there. Over the years I have heard countless variations of practitioners' experiences. To understand their experience with natural awareness, each one maps it against their own life experience; cultural, religious, and spiritual views; and ways they make sense of the world.

So is resting in a place of natural awareness accessing Buddha nature? Or Christ consciousness, or Grandmother spirit, or the Divine, or the Mystery? Or is it our brain entering theta waves and creating synchrony?

I think the answer is, nobody really knows. Everyone, including you (and the blind men with the elephant), will try to understand their experience of natural awareness on the basis of how they construct the world, and my encouragement is to please trust your own interpretations and to seek support from teachers when it's hard to make sense of something.

Practice accessing natural awareness and see what happens. How do you feel during the practice? What kind of effect does it have on your life? Is it leading to more peace, compassion, and wisdom? Then, however you choose to describe it, natural awareness may be worth a deeper look.

Personally, I often find that the phrases "the nature of mind" or "resting in awakened awareness" create a deep relaxation, joy, and openness of mind for me. I take these phrases to be metaphors, and I love them. I play with them to enhance my experiential understanding of natural awareness. If you find using these phrases—or similar metaphorical, spiritual, or religious language—helps you shift from identification with your dramas into something much vaster and more peaceful, then the metaphors are doing their job. When we're no longer caught in the grasping, we're open to deep peace, profound clarity, and the possibility of boundless compassion.

Will we ever discover if natural awareness is our true nature, or the nature of everything, or . . . ? It's hard to say, but I'm not holding my breath. Those metaphors may feel subjectively right, and they may be what some religious traditions tell us, but ultimately no one can ever prove if they are an accurate description of reality. To me, that's absolutely fine. I like living in the Mystery.

11 ❧ THE MULTIFACETED DIAMOND

Natural awareness is not just one experience but many. So let's use some more metaphors to point to natural awareness. What I will share is purely subjective, based on my own and my students' accounts. Some students describe similar qualities arising in classical mindfulness, so I won't say natural awareness corners the market on these states. What students do report is that natural awareness practice often provides quicker access to these states, and often with less effort, than classical mindfulness practice.

Sometimes natural awareness is just that: a sense of being naturally aware, here and now, without much, if any, effort. But often it is coarising with certain qualities or flavors. Here's a metaphor: We can think of natural awareness as being like an exquisite, giant diamond with hundreds of facets. Imagine now that each shining facet has a different quality or flavor, and each time you use a natural awareness practice, it is as if you turn the diamond and illuminate a new facet. These qualities/facets may not be illuminated in your initial glimpses of natural awareness, but as you gain facility with natural awareness practices, they become more discernable. They show up more frequently and sustain themselves over longer period of times.

Some of the facets I have experienced in my own practice include a feeling of deep peace, unquestionable interconnection, a heartfelt sense of love, a sense of transcendence, a fullness, an emptiness, a feeling of broken-hearted compassion for the world, a sense of deep ease, a blissed-out feeling, tears of joy, a feeling of pure equanimity or even-mindedness, contentment, a light sweetness, a vulnerability, and a poignancy. Sometimes tears come in the midst of the experience. I've had several experiences of pure hilarity when I could not stop laughing, as if I were in on some great cosmic joke. Sometimes I experience a sense of utter ordinariness and just here-ness. Awareness is present, and my mind simply knows life as it unfolds. Often natural awareness feels like a kind of transparency, like my sense of self is so reduced that I am part of everything.

Natural awareness can be or include any of these qualities. And many other facets always emerge, as natural awareness is an endlessly creative field. And most interestingly, each person experiences this diamond in different ways, as if the light of luminosity is refracted uniquely through each individual. This luminosity also comes in varying degrees, just as on a spectrum, from subtle, a whisper of, to just is, full on, almost overwhelming, fully formed.

Whatever your experience is, it will be just that—*your* experience.

A QUOTE

One of my favorite ways to access natural awareness is through quotes or poetry that point to the state. Sometimes just reading or repeating a quote can allow a softening in my body and a relaxation into easeful awareness.

Once you are settled, drop the following quote into a receptive mind and notice the effects. You might repeat it several times during one meditation session.

> Having purified the great delusion,
> the heart's darkness, the radiant light
> of the unobscured sun continually rises.
> DUDJOM LINGPA RINPOCHE[1]

12 \ DEVELOPING A NATURAL AWARENESS PRACTICE

Developing our natural awareness practice is a process. We begin by understanding the foundations, which leads to our cultivating it through meditation and then moves us toward embodying it in all of life.

First, we are exposed to the idea of natural awareness. We learn how it operates, what helps cultivate it, and why it might be useful to pursue. We might read about it or listen to natural awareness teachings. We might recognize the moments of natural awareness that we have experienced in our lives—when we are engaging with nature, in sports, in creative pursuits—and wonder how these beautiful moments might be accessed, cultivated, and sustained.

Since natural awareness is not merely a theory, our next step is to explore meditative approaches to accessing natural awareness. If we already have a classical mindfulness meditation practice, we begin incorporating natural awareness practice into it. We might also use informal practices, like glimpse practices and mental shifts (which we'll discuss in part II). Slowly we gain more comfort with natural awareness. In our classical mindfulness meditation practice, we notice a shift into more ease and openness, and most of us continue to practice classical mindfulness meditation as well, perhaps mixing the two practices.

Once we feel the benefit of meditating with natural awareness, we may want to experience it throughout the day. Right at the moment I wrote this sentence, I looked outside and saw the pinkish sunset clouds above me. I softened my body, felt my back body, and settled my mind for a moment. A feeling of contentment rose over me, pervading my typing.

So once you have the hang of accessing natural awareness and have experience meditating with it, you can bring natural awareness to your mind and make shifts into it during your daily life as often as you remember to and feel drawn to. It doesn't matter if your experience of natural awareness lasts three seconds or three minutes or three hours; what's important is that you begin to incorporate moments of natural awareness into your day, throughout the day. I'll discuss integrating natural awareness into our daily life in much more detail in part III.

What people usually notice is that through understanding the foundations, learning natural awareness meditation, using glimpse practices to access natural awareness, and incorporating it into life, natural awareness starts to become a default setting. Often natural awareness spontaneously arises for us at surprising moments. We begin to embody it. It's a rare person who lives in natural awareness entirely every moment. Most of us flow in and out of it. But touching it again and again has a deep impact on our sense of self, and we slowly start to live from it.

Keep in mind that exploring natural awareness as a three-stage process—understand, practice, embody—is an ideal. Often our journey with natural awareness is a lot less linear. We are in a honeymoon phase when we first learn about it, but then we get discouraged or distracted, and our daily meditation practice dwindles. Then we go on a meditation retreat and get reinvigorated and feel like we "got" something. And for some months or longer we notice how natural awareness seems so close by and easily accessible. Then life throws up a roadblock: we get sick or lose our job or end a relationship, and natural awareness feels a million miles away. And then we recommit and read and study and practice intensively for a period of time, deepening our understanding and experience.

You get the picture: natural awareness practice is a lifetime practice. I love that, because it means the pressure is off. No matter what life brings, if we set out to access natural awareness with a clear intention, we will continue to move in its direction in a beautiful nonlinear fashion, which is wholly in keeping with how life works—bumpy, unsystematic, mysterious, and always surprising.

13 ◆ LIVING FROM NATURAL AWARENESS

From time to time I hear of people who experience unremitting natural awareness over long periods of time, and they claim that it is their permanent state. This is amazing, but it is rare.

For most serious practitioners, natural awareness comes and goes, and yet it can feel like the ground of who we are, even if it's just background awareness. Slowly, we begin to embody it, and, as I mentioned in the previous chapter, it becomes our default setting.

When natural awareness becomes the default, students describe more transparency, less identification with thoughts, quicker turnaround time with strong emotions, a greater sense of spaciousness, less self-centeredness, more compassion toward themselves and others, more ease, and profound well-being. Of course, living from natural awareness is a nonlinear process. Most everyone spirals in and out of it throughout a lifetime.

Since you're probably wondering, I'll tell you that I do not live every moment in a state of natural awareness. But I would say that natural awareness lies at the depth of my being. My default tendency is sometimes reactive at first, but then often, when I can settle my mind, I can access a place inside myself that knows contentment. I certainly get caught in my petty dramas and worries and so forth, but as long as I practice, I almost always can come back to a place of equilibrium. I almost always can have a sense of spaciousness with the drama, although finding it may take some time. I feel deep inside myself a sense of okay-ness, and I relate to others from this understanding. A desire to serve someone feels more prominent than a desire to use or gain from them. My heart is geared toward compassion.

And I still get worried that my daughter won't get into a good college (she's eight). I still get irritated by various family members who shall not be named. I still feel anxious when work feels overwhelming. I still want to scream when faced with the current political situation and often do. I still forget to close the kitchen cabinet doors in spite of ongoing reminders. My mind tends to worry, and I have to check that quite a bit. I'm pretty normal, I have to say.

The difference is simply this: I have reliably effective tools for pulling me away from the reactivity and emotional distress and into a place of ease. I have no doubt in my mind's capacity to find freedom, even if it takes a little time. And more deeply, I feel like I live with an underlying sense of abiding well-being and trust in my own goodness, which is present even when I blow it, or get anxious, or lose it. Natural awareness is available to me at any moment. Sometimes it sustains throughout much of the day; sometimes it's more of a whisper. Whenever I remember to connect with it, natural awareness or just plain old mindfulness is there for me. I can shift my mind at any moment. Natural awareness feels like the baseline of who I am.

14 ❧ A CAVEAT
DON'T BE A BLISS NINNY

The ability to tap into our own natural awareness, and the sense that "all is well" that often accompanies it, does not negate the reality of our lives or of the world outside us.

We practitioners can delude ourselves into thinking, *That's it. I've got something. Now my life is always going to be good, and I don't have to worry about anything outside of myself. The world may be messed up, but I know fundamentally all is well.*

This point of view is not optimal.

Life, in my experience, is a profound mix of joy and sorrow. We have good days and bad days; we have gains and losses all the time. I recently drove through a red light. Well, it was yellow when I accelerated. And it was at one of those camera intersections, so I'll be looking forward to a hefty fine and traffic school. This is life. We fight with our spouses and children. We get overwhelmed by work or family responsibilities.

And beyond the day-to-day ups and downs, sometimes our lives are filled with tragedy. We get sick. People we love get sick and sometimes die. Marriages end. People betray us. We're broke. Or we live under conditions of violence or poverty. Or people we care about live under these conditions.

Meanwhile, there is tremendous suffering on the planet. Wars, famine, illnesses, economic crises, ecological disasters, polarization of the rich and the poor, human trafficking— well, you know, the list goes on and on.

It seems to be the nature of the human condition that we live with a relentless mixture of joy and sorrow. The world has incredible examples of beauty and unremitting examples of violence and despair.

So the question is, if I access natural awareness and it becomes a part of me, will all these things go away?

No, they will not.

It is a mistake to think that because we have access to a deeper peace, suddenly we will live in goodness and joy all the time, and things will always go right. I have to resurrect a term from the 1970s: *bliss ninny*. It means someone who saunters around in some apparent spiritual, blissed out, holier-than-thou state. It's someone whose response to personal or worldly suffering is "It's all good" or "It's meant to be." Even worse are the bliss ninnies who think they are above ethical constraints. They ignore basic ethics because "It all doesn't matter" or "It's all good." (We'll get into ethics in chapter 66.)

Bliss ninnies have it all wrong. Here's what is a bit more realistic: When we have an understanding of natural awareness, begin to access it, and from time to time live connected to it, we can and often do experience a profound underlying sense of well-being. But we are also mature enough to understand the paradox: While goodness exists, both inside and out of us, the suffering of the world is part of life, too. We are not in denial of that reality.

An ability to be mindful and aware allows us to handle whatever life brings with aplomb, equanimity, and even a sense of humor about things (which is what eventually arose about my traffic ticket, but believe me, it took a few days). It is a tool for accessing our inherent goodness, and doing so reminds us that, deep down, we know we can handle life. Understanding that we have access to natural awareness shows us that even when life's problems seem insurmountable, we will get through them somehow.

The suffering of the world can break your heart—and that's on a good day. Sometimes life's challenges are so overwhelming, all we can do is live through them, bearing each day the best we can. But accessing our natural awareness can help us manage despair. Practicing natural awareness is in no way about passivity. In the face of injustice or personal or global suffering, natural awareness can connect us to our inner resources and open our heart to compassion. It can motivate us to act with awareness, even-mindedness, wisdom, and love, rather than from a place of disempowerment, rage, fear, or grief. This is the promise of awareness.

BANK OF A RIVER ANALOGY

This practice is an invocation of an analogy. Read it slowly and let the image sink in—not to dwell on it, but to see how it impacts your consciousness. Take in the analogy as you settle into your own sense of being. Keep it in the back of your mind throughout a meditation session or at any point in the day.

Imagine you are sitting on the bank of a flowing river. The water is rushing past. You can't put your hand in and grasp the river, because it is ever flowing. Leaves, sticks, stones, and other debris flow by, carried on the current. These objects are like our thoughts, memories, images, and worries—all floating by as we sit on the bank, just noticing them.

PART II

TECHNIQUES

MEDITATING WITH NATURAL AWARENESS

15 \ MEDITATION PRACTICE BASICS

You may already have a classical mindfulness meditation practice. If you don't and you want to get started, here are some simple guidelines.

When?

Pick a time of day that will work for your life. Don't assume you have to meditate in the morning; night owls will never sustain a morning practice. Some people meditate when they wake up, and others practice at night before going to bed; still others do it when they come home from work or school. The best time to meditate is the time that will work best for *you*.

How Long?

The amount of time can vary. I generally start students with just five minutes and work them up to twenty to thirty minutes. I'd rather you start with a short, doable stretch than have you attempt a longer stretch right away and then get discouraged when you can't sustain it.

Where?

Find a place in your home that works as a meditation spot for you. It could be a room or a corner of a room. It just needs to be a place you're unlikely to be disturbed. If you designate it as your meditation spot, your mind will get habituated to it, so that when, for example, you sit in a particular chair, your mind automatically gears up to meditate. You might want to decorate your spot with meaningful art, photographs, or objects from nature, but this is not necessary.

How Do I Sit?

You can sit in a chair or cross-legged on a cushion on the floor. But please remember there is nothing particularly holy about being able to sit on the floor. Most of our students at UCLA meditate in chairs. Find a posture that will be supportive to you, that generally keeps your back upright, and that is comfortable enough to sustain for the duration of your meditation.

If you have physical challenges, you may have to experiment with your meditation posture. You can try lying down, standing up, or alternating between several postures.

I have to say that my favorite posture for natural awareness practice is sitting in a comfy overstuffed chair with a view of my backyard. I put a few pillows behind my back to keep my torso upright. And I'll confess, on really lazy days I do lazy meditation: propping myself upright in bed with a few pillows. I don't even have to get out of bed to get started. The upright posture can support our meditation, so we can't take posture too lightly, but I'm also of the "whatever works" school of meditation.

How Often?

You want to meditate on a regular basis. Aim for daily practice—even if it's just five minutes daily. But if it ends up being three or four times a week or less, that's fine. Start where you are. Set an intention to meditate more frequently the following week. Developing a habit is hard work, no matter what it is, as I discovered when I tried to stop eating sugar. You definitely don't want to beat yourself up for not practicing. As you practice over time and start to see results in your life, you will usually be drawn to more consistency, as well as longer duration, in your practice.

16 \ CLARIFYING AND SETTING INTENTIONS

I rarely meditate without first reflecting a bit on my intentions and then setting my motivation for the practice session. This process puts me in touch with my deeper commitment to myself and the practice.

If you wish to try this, you can begin with a reflection: "Why am I practicing today?" Be willing to accept any answer that arises inside you, ranging from "Because I know it's good for me" to "Because I'm supposed to do it every day" to "Because it helps relieve stress" to "Because it puts me in touch with my own deepest longings for truth and connection."

We don't need to judge our motivation; we just need to get to know ourselves. Sometimes my crabby response to myself is "Just because—and stop asking!" Other times it's "Because it's what I deeply love." Often this simple reflection gives me a little juice to get going.

Then it's helpful to set your motivation—that is, to deliberately state to yourself what your practice is about, what kind of intention you hold. This intention could be anything meaningful to you: To wake up more fully in life. To live with more wisdom and compassion. To serve people. To open your heart. To find a deeper peace. To live day to day in more awareness. Sometimes I say: "May this practice be a cause and condition for waking up and benefiting others." If that sounds too lofty, you can keep it simple: "May I practice wholeheartedly." "May I open to awareness." "May I be kind."

Some people like to connect their motivation setting to others in the world, recognizing that they are practicing not just for themselves, but for the benefit of everyone, no exceptions. Transforming our own minds impacts our families, work, friends, neighborhoods, communities, and the institutions of which we are a part. So we can see our own meditation practice in a vast web of connections, which can be quite inspiring.

Feel free to use whatever you're drawn to. Maybe try these intentions: "Make me an instrument of your peace" (attributed to Saint Francis of Assisi) or "Grant me the serenity to accept the things I cannot change, the courage to change the things I can, and the wisdom to know the difference" (Reinhold Niebuhr).

This practice of clarifying and setting intentions is completely optional. Try it and see how it affects your meditation. If you find it helpful and inspiring, keep going with it. If not, no need to continue. One added benefit is if you're going through a difficult time in meditation or in life, you can always return to your motivation to help you get through.

At the end of a practice session, some people find it helpful to reconnect with their motivation, set a motivation for the day, and even share the power of their practice with others. If you feel like you've generated positive benefit from meditating, you can imagine that benefit radiating out into the world.

ASK YOURSELF . . .

Here's a question to ask yourself to help you access natural awareness. It is not meant for you to analyze and ruminate on but, rather, for you to simply drop into your receptive mind.

So get centered, relax, and try some breath awareness to calm your mind in meditation. Or in daily life, take a breath or two and then drop the following question into your mind, as if dropping a stone into a pond to notice the ripples. Listen deeply and see what emerges.

**What is here now if there
is no problem to solve?**
ATTRIBUTED TO LOCH KELLY

17 ❧ CLASSICAL MINDFULNESS MEDITATION
FOCUSED AWARENESS PRACTICE

Chapters 17 through 19 offer classical mindfulness meditation instructions for those of you who are newer and don't feel quite ready to jump into natural awareness practice. First I will describe the practice, and then I will offer instructions you can use to try it yourself.

Classical mindfulness meditation generally starts with a focused awareness practice to help calm and stabilize our mind. Most of us have busy and easily distracted minds. Focused awareness practice is an excellent starting point, as it cultivates concentration to help unify and tame our busy minds. Concentration can also lead to more clarity. (For more about the value of concentration, see chapter 29.)

To practice focused awareness, I encourage students to feel their breath in their body, specifically where they sense the breath most clearly—the abdomen, chest, or nose. I ask them to notice what physical sensations the breath produces in that part of the body, such as rising, falling, expansion, contraction, coolness, tingling, temperature changes, or slight movement.

Then I ask students to choose one area—the abdomen, chest, or nose—where the breath is the easiest, clearest, or most interesting to notice, and I tell them to try to maintain their attention on that area by feeling their breath as it moves through it. We can call what a meditator focuses on a *meditation anchor*. Like a ship's anchor, which keeps a ship from being tossed and turned in the waves, a meditation anchor keeps our minds from being tossed and turned by the turbulent waves of thoughts and emotions, because it is something we can always return to.

Some people have a hard time feeling their breath or realize that their breath is not "neutral"—meaning, they have some reaction to it. Maybe they have a cold, or their breath seems elusive or even uncomfortable. In that case, I recommend that they listen to the ambient sounds of the room as the sounds come and go.[1] Whatever their chosen anchor, the aim is to keep their attention on it.

At some point, their attention is pulled away into who knows what—stories, memories, plans, worries, fantasies, and so on. This is what minds do. It's not a problem, nor does it mean the students are doing the meditation wrong. The moment they notice that their attention has drifted *is a moment of awareness*.

In that moment, I tell them, they are to gently direct their attention back to their main focus. Mentally saying a soft cue word, like *thinking* or *wandering*, helps them make the shift.

You can try this focused awareness practice for yourself by following these instructions:

Once you are settled in a comfortable posture, notice your full body seated. Take a breath or two to help encourage relaxation. You can close your eyes, unless for some reason that doesn't feel comfortable to you.

Gently turn your attention to the sensations of breathing in your body. You may feel your abdomen rising and falling, your chest expanding and contracting, or the air moving through your nose. Try this for a minute or so.

Then let go of attending to your breath and turn your attention to the sounds around you that are coming and going. Listen to them as if you were listening to your favorite music. Try not to get caught in a story or reaction about the sounds. Just listen.

For a meditation anchor, choose to focus either on your breath moving in one of the physical areas I mentioned or on the sounds around you. Whichever you choose, try to notice breath after breath or sound after sound.

When you notice that your attention has wandered, you can say a soft word in your mind, like *thinking* or *wandering*, and gently redirect your attention back to your breath or the listening. Keep returning to your anchor whenever you notice your mind has wandered.

Try to sustain this practice for a short period of time. Conclude the meditation when you are ready and feel the impact of meditating on your body and mind.

When we get started with classical mindfulness meditation, our minds are usually pretty untamed, restless, and lost in thinking. It may seem like we can stay focused on our anchor for only a second or two—and even those moments of focus are rare. But over time we will find that our ability to focus improves, and the duration of focus lengthens. It's almost like a muscle; if you work out, your muscle will get stronger over time. In the same way, if you practice focusing, your ability to focus will strengthen over time.

18 ❧ CLASSICAL MINDFULNESS MEDITATION EXPANDED
FLEXIBLE AWARENESS PRACTICE

Once we have more stability in our meditation, we will find that classical mindfulness can go beyond merely attending to our anchor in order to cultivate a focused awareness. We can progress into bringing awareness to whatever is happening (such as a sensation, thought, or emotion) when it becomes obvious. Our attention is becoming more flexible toward objects.

For example, say that you're meditating with your breath as your anchor, and a body sensation—like an overpowering itch—arises. It feels more obvious than your breathing. So you turn your attention to the itch. Don't return your attention immediately to your breath. Instead, purposely feel the itch—noticing how it changes—until it no longer holds your attention, it has stopped, or your attention has shifted onto something else. Then you might return your attention to your breathing.

As you continue meditating, you can let your attention follow anything new that grabs it. You might follow a train of thoughts or a set of emotions as it moves through you. After a while, you will find that sometimes your attention is focused on your anchor, and sometimes it is focused on "secondary objects." And your attention will probably move flexibly between the two focuses. You investigate the object, noticing its changing and insubstantial nature.

Try it for yourself.

Begin your meditation in a comfortable posture. Close your eyes, if you wish, and take a few breaths to help you settle. Then try a few minutes of focused awareness practice.

Connect with your anchor: feel your breathing or listen to sounds. When thoughts take you away from your anchor, notice you have wandered and then return again to your anchor. Try this for a few minutes.

Now that your mind is more concentrated, you can notice when your attention strays from your anchor. But instead of bringing it back right away, keep your attention on whatever is grabbing it—the achy back, the blaring siren, the funny thought. Sense, feel, notice, or listen to whatever has pulled your attention away from your anchor.

When the new object no longer holds your attention, return your attention to your anchor. Then stay with your anchor until something else pulls your attention away. Fully notice, sense, or feel the new object until your attention moves back to your anchor or to another new object.

Keep practicing in this manner for as long as you feel drawn to. When you are ready to stop, notice the impact of the meditation and open your eyes.

Sometimes you may find that you let go of your anchor entirely and your attention is drawn to one secondary object after another. When that happens, you're engaging more fully in "flexible awareness." Chapter 19 will explore fully flexible awareness in more detail.

BACK-BODY AWARENESS

For most of us, our attention is usually focused forward. We see what is in front of us, and unless we have back pain, we might ignore the back of our body. This glimpse practice has us notice our back body. By opening our senses in a way that is not typical for us, we can often find ourselves dropping into a more aware state.

Take a few breaths to stabilize your mind. Become aware of your body, noticing whatever sensations are obvious to you in this moment—heaviness, lightness, tingling, warmth, and so on.

Turn your attention now to the back of your body. What can you feel along the back of your body? Similar sensations of warmth, hardness, pressure? Soften and unclench your belly. Rest there with an investigative mind, letting yourself feel sensations with curiosity. You may find that a simultaneous awareness arises in your full body. You may find yourself relaxing more as you begin to include your back body in your awareness. Notice if your awareness settles or expands. Observe what happens for you.

19 \ CLASSICAL MINDFULNESS MEDITATION EXPANDED FURTHER
FULLY FLEXIBLE AWARENESS PRACTICE

Flexible awareness practice is one of the stops on the spectrum of awareness practices (see chapter 7). I often teach it in conjunction with practices for accessing natural awareness, because flexible awareness includes elements of both focused awareness and natural awareness. Flexible awareness practice is another part of classical mindfulness meditation.

In a fully flexible awareness practice, we don't have an anchor or central focus to our meditation, but instead move our attention among secondary objects (such as sounds, the breath, thoughts, sensations, or emotions), noticing them on the basis of which one is calling out to us or which one is most obvious. So, for instance, you might notice a memory, then a vibration on your hand, then a sound, then a breath, then a feeling of frustration. The frustration may appear first as a thought, but then suddenly you notice heat in your belly. And so on. You can flexibly move your attention to whatever object is calling out to you, whichever object you choose.

One of the benefits to flexible awareness practice is that when we turn our attention to secondary objects, we investigate their nature. We discover that although they seem permanent and solid, they are actually changing and insubstantial.

Sometimes we experience being aware of objects without seeming to choose them. We find ourselves attending fairly effortlessly and spontaneously to whatever is calling out for our attention, moment by moment. We can call this experience *choiceless awareness*—meaning we don't choose the objects, but they choose us! In advanced states of meditation, we can experience the rapid flow of arising and disappearing objects and have enough awareness to be present to all of them as they speed by.

Let's give it a try.

 Get in a comfortable posture. Close your eyes, if you wish, and begin with some focused awareness to help calm your mind. Focus on your breathing, and when your attention wanders off, bring it back to your breathing. Or if sound is your anchor, you can listen to the sounds around you.

Although you are attending to your anchor, it is likely that other things are happening in the background—meaning they are occurring, but you are not focusing on them. Now let the background become foreground. Notice whatever grabs your attention: you hear a sound, and you just listen to it; you notice a strong sensation in your body, and you feel it; a memory arises, and you notice the image or thought; another sensation comes, and you feel it; and so on. You can choose where to place your attention, or let the objects choose you, bringing attention to whatever is most obvious in any given moment.

You may start to feel a little lost without your anchor, so if you feel unsure about what to notice, go back to your anchor at any point. After a while try letting go of your anchor again and tuning in to whatever objects arise in your mind, from moment to moment.

Practice for as long as you feel drawn to. Whenever you are ready to stop, notice the effect of the practice on your body and mind, and when you are ready, open your eyes or conclude the meditation.

Flexible Awareness of Mental Activity

An interesting variation of flexible awareness is being flexibly aware only of our mental activity. Many students enjoy this type of practice, which we might think of as simply "noticing our mind." You can settle back and turn your attention to whatever is arising in your mental field—thoughts, emotions, moods, and mental states. You notice what's arising and, if you wish, label it—*planning*, *remembering*, *judging*, *worrying*, *imagining*, and so forth. I sometimes imagine a little person crawling into my head and bearing witness to what's going on there.

This practice is actually a lot of fun if you have sufficient concentration to do it. You will know you have the necessary concentration because it feels fairly easy to keep your attention focused on your anchor without too much wandering.

Here, give it a try.

 Settle into a comfortable physical position. Close your eyes, if you wish. Using your breathing or listening to sounds, spend a few minutes using focused awareness practice to stabilize your mind.

When you are ready, let go of your breath and any other physical or external object of focus, and turn your attention to your mind. See if you can notice thought after thought after thought. Give them labels, if it is helpful, such as *planning, remembering, worrying, fantasizing, judging.*

What happens when you notice a thought? Does it disappear? Can you think the thought with awareness? Do you notice a thought at the beginning, middle, or end of the thought?

Have fun with the exploration. If you start to feel overwhelmed or lost, take a break by bringing awareness to a physical aspect of your meditation: your bodily sensations or your breath. Or return to your anchor. Notice the physical sensations for a little while until you can return your attention to the mental activity.

If you are enjoying this practice, stay with it as long as you are drawn to. If it feels challenging, do it for just a few minutes at a time. Once you stop, notice the effect on your body and mind and then conclude the meditation.

20 ❧ SHIFT INTO NATURAL AWARENESS

Okay, we have the basics of classical mindfulness meditation down. Now let's look at three deliberate mental shifts you can make during classical mindfulness meditation that should help point you toward natural awareness: relaxing effort, broadening attention, and dropping objects.

Relaxing Effort

Using effort in classical mindfulness meditation typically means working to bring our attention back to whatever is the present-moment experience. We rigorously and faithfully return our attention to our main focus, typically our breathing. The moment we notice we've gotten lost in thought, we deliberately redirect our attention back to our breathing. It can be very hard work. I've seen meditators covered in sweat, straining to be aware.

This type of overexertion in meditation is too extreme. In classical mindfulness meditation, we need to be balanced between effort that leads to clear seeing and too much effort that doesn't really serve us. Some meditators experience a lot of self-judgment, believing that they're not trying hard enough.

Classical mindfulness meditators typically report that focusing gets easier over time. They can stay aware of their breathing for extended periods, or they find that they return their attention to their breath more quickly when it wanders away.

Some people call this ease *effortless effort*—an experience in our meditation practice where we are making an effort, but it doesn't seem hard to do at all.

Relaxing effort to shift into natural awareness is a little different. It means that we rein in the tendency to try to put our attention on our breath or other objects, and instead we just *be* with the objects as they arise.

I think a common concern of many meditators is that if they stop trying, then nothing will happen. Meditators also worry that their mind will wander all over the place if they are not making any effort to do something with it. Well, just sitting down and not doing anything wouldn't be natural awareness practice; it would be sitting down and doing nothing. So that's not what we're trying to do here. Dropping or relaxing effort is very different in that we are tuning in to the awareness that is already present, without trying hard to get there. We also don't necessarily have a wandering mind because we relax effort on the heels of having worked hard to pay attention.

Think of shifting into natural awareness like riding a bicycle. Often we pedal really hard, but at a certain point, we stop pedaling and begin coasting. The bike stays upright, and we continue to head wherever we're going, but we're not working so hard. In fact, it's usually quite exhilarating to coast on a bicycle. The coasting is dependent upon the earlier pedaling stage, just like effortlessness in meditation is dependent upon the effort you made earlier—particularly the effort to concentrate your mind.

So what does relaxing effort feel like in meditation? It feels like stopping the attempt to wrestle with your unruly mind, to bring it effortfully back to the present, and instead resting, relaxing, and exploring the awareness that is already present. It often feels like things are just happening on their own, and we're witnessing them. It can feel immensely relaxing and joyful to stop the struggle. We may lose the effortlessness, and then it takes a bit of effort to return to it (such as deliberately returning our attention to our breath for a few moments—or, to return to our bicycle analogy, pedaling for a block or two), but for the most part we are coasting, not pedaling. This relaxing of effort is one way to access a natural awareness.

Try it now.

 Start your meditation session by closing your eyes, if you wish, and taking about ten minutes to develop focus and calm by rigorously paying attention to your breathing. When your attention wanders, bring it back to your breathing with regularity and precision.

After ten minutes, see if you can simply pause the effort you are making. Relax a bit (and that may include relaxing your body), and notice what is happening without you trying to be aware. Is awareness present? Are you naturally aware of what is happening in your body or mind, without deliberately placing your attention on the object? Can you sense the way awareness is happening, kind of on its own, and how you are present without having to work at it?

If you notice yourself getting lost in thoughts, then make an effort to come back to your breath for a while. But then stop making an effort again and see what happens.

Broadening Attention

Your attention can be very narrowly focused or broadly focused. It can also be somewhere in between. You might notice the differences because you naturally adjust the breadth of your attention in life all the time. You are driving your car, and you focus first on your dashboard, and then you automatically shift to a wider peripheral sense of the road in front of you. You are talking with a friend, and you focus on her face, then shift to her whole body, and then notice the room in which you both are sitting.

We can think of the mechanism of attention as being like a camera. Sometimes you use a telescopic lens in order to focus on something quite narrow—maybe taking a close-up of a flower, seeing the intricacies of the stem and petals in detail. Usually we take midrange photos—of our kids, friends at the game, or whatever the selfie du jour is—employing a lens that is not too narrowly focused, but open in a general way. The far end of the spectrum would be when we use a panoramic lens to take an elongated, comprehensive photo of, let's say, the Grand Canyon.

When we meditate, we can apply a narrow or panoramic attention. An example of using a narrow focus would be attending primarily to your breath (or any single object of focus). The panoramic attention would be when our attention is wide open—when we notice many things going on or just have a general wide view. When, for example, we listen to sounds coming from all directions surrounding us, this is a panoramic attention, or wide focus.

We can even apply an attention in meditation that's somewhere in between these two. A somewhere-in-between attention might be when a few things are going on and our attention can encompass them, either simultaneously or consecutively. Our lower back is achy, and we're trying to attend to the pain. And then perhaps we move our attention to a global sense of our body or to a part of our body that feels okay at the moment (typically our hands or feet), so that we're not overwhelmed by the pain (this is a helpful recommendation if you're experiencing pain in meditation).

Broad, panoramic attention tends to be the type of attention present when we do natural awareness practice. Because most of us gravitate toward a focused attention both in meditation and in daily life, opening up panoramically can actually invite in natural awareness. It counteracts our usual forward-focus tendencies and allows our minds to rest and reset, kind of like a brain vacation.

But broad or panoramic attention *does not equal* natural awareness; instead, shifting into broad attention will point us *in the direction of* natural awareness. That's why many of the glimpse practices in this book focus on broadening our attention. Sometimes as we practice broadening our attention, we find ourselves thoroughly and completely aware, which is close to how I defined *natural awareness* earlier in the book. And it is also possible to have natural awareness without noticing broadly.

Try broadening your attention right now.

Close your eyes if that is comfortable to you. Start by narrowing your attention to a single area of focus in your body—your abdomen, chest, or nostrils. Try to keep this narrow focus for a few minutes.

Now begin to listen to the sounds around you. Start with sounds nearby, but then listen with an expansive ear. How far away are the sounds you can hear? Listen to the sound that is farthest out. Try this approach to listening for a minute or two.

Now notice your whole body. Can you fully feel your body seated here? Relax and unclench your belly. Imagine you could expand that sense of your body, feeling your body moving out in all directions, including above and below. Try being aware of your expanded body for another minute.

Finally, open your eyes and let your gaze become peripheral—wide open, noticing the space around you. Let your eyes be soft, but take in an expansive view. Keep your stomach relaxed. Explore this expanded view for a few minutes, resting here, and then notice what happens to your awareness.

Dropping Objects

When you're practicing classical mindfulness meditation, probably the most important shift you can make to invite in natural awareness is to move your attention from objects to objectless-ness. Now what on earth does that mean?

Objects of meditation are, simply put, the things we focus on, such as the breath, body sensations, emotions, thoughts. An object can also be something outside us, like another person, sights, or sounds. Any kind of thing can be an object of meditation. Taking something as the object of our awareness is basic to classical mindfulness meditation, as you saw in the previous chapters. Focusing on objects and attending to them is generally how we live our life as well.

Object*less* awareness, typically developed in meditation and uncommon in daily life, is when we focus less on the objects of awareness and instead focus on the *awareness itself.* There will be objects arising in our meditation—thoughts, emotions, sensations, for example—but since they are not the focus, they are less distinct, and we become aware of awareness itself. So instead of our anchor being our breath, for example, our anchor is awareness itself.

People tend to experience objectless awareness in three different ways: that in which everything is contained, that which knows, and that which just is.

That in which everything is contained. Broadening attention from a narrow focus to a more panoramic perception is closely aligned with the experience of objectless awareness as that in which everything is contained. You will notice me using analogies like "Our mind is like the sky, and everything in it is like clouds floating by." This helps me convey the idea that awareness contains everything. So when we turn our attention to the sky-like nature of our mind, noticing the boundless space around things, we are noticing the field of awareness in which everything is contained. Some people experience objectless awareness in this way.

Remember the window analogy from chapter 7? In the third way of noticing, we looked out the window and took in the full view in a relaxed way. Rather than specifically focusing on individual vehicles, we could somehow be aware of everything that was happening simultaneously, and our vision seemed to contain everything.

That which knows. The second idea that objectless awareness focuses on is a little tricky. Most of us are used to focusing on objects when we meditate, but what happens when we make the shift to noticing that which is being aware—to seeking the knower? Oftentimes this shift can feel quite joyful and freeing. Many of the practices in the book move us toward awareness of awareness, as you will see. If you start searching for the knower, what do you find?

The idea is that we can notice things, and we also notice the thing that notices things. We can take our attention from an outward focus on objects and turn it inward, as if we are reversing our attention—trying to move from that which we are aware of to that which is aware of what we are aware of.

One of my colleagues, Daniel J. Siegel, uses a concept called the "Wheel of Awareness" to explain awareness of awareness.[1] The center hub of the wheel is awareness (that which knows), and on the rim are all the possible things we can pay attention to: input from the five senses, inner awareness, thoughts, emotions, and external objects. He takes students through awareness of all of these different domains, sending "spokes of awareness" out from the hub to the rim. Then he asks students to turn the spokes back in on themselves to become aware of the hub—which is awareness, that which knows.

So awareness is essentially knowing itself. You've turned from the objects of awareness to the awareness itself.

That which just is. Sometimes in objectless awareness we turn our attention to awareness itself, and it is neither that which contains everything nor that which knows, but is more like a deep felt sense that we are aware. We are here. We are fully present, and everything seems to be happening on its own. This way of experiencing awareness can often surprise you, but it may feel like the awareness is unshakable, that it spontaneously is present, and that there is not much you can do to stop being aware. No matter what is happening, including thoughts, we are fully and uncompromisingly aware.

Let's give objectless awareness a try. Please trust your intuition about whether or not you have shifted into objectless awareness. And keep in mind that it may take time for you to become confident about whether or not you have made this shift.

The following meditation will lead you through all three ways of experiencing objectless awareness.

 Close your eyes and spend a few minutes practicing awareness of your breathing to stabilize and calm your mind.

Now open your eyes and notice the visual field in front of you. See if you can notice panoramically, taking in the full field.

Then notice that there are visual objects in front of you. But can you become aware of the space around the objects rather than the objects themselves? Imagine that your mind is like the sky and your thoughts are just like clouds passing by. If this makes sense, can you make the leap into noticing the space, not just in front of you, but also in your mind—the sky-like nature of your mind in which everything is contained?

Now let's shift to a new exploration. Look out at your experience. Start visually: Notice the visual field in front of you. You are aware of sights.

Now redirect your attention to that which is seeing. What do you find? Some part of you is knowing your thoughts. Who is the knower?

As you continue your meditation, awareness is present. Can you find that part of you that is aware? Don't try to figure this out conceptually; instead, what do you experience? Ask the question "Who is aware?" and see what your inner response is.

Last exploration: What if you were to simply be here? No agenda, nothing to do, nowhere to go. Just be. Everything is happening on its own. What would be here if you didn't have a problem to solve? If nothing was wrong?

Of these three explorations, maybe one of them makes sense to you, and the others don't land.

If so, please continue on with the one that makes sense.

Continue practicing for a few minutes, letting your attention rest in whatever state you have evoked throughout these practices.

Once you understand how to shift into natural awareness by relaxing effort, broadening attention, or dropping the focus on objects, you can then practice natural awareness meditation, which will invite these experiences to deepen and be sustained.

NOTICE THE NOTICER

Who's being aware? This is the perennial meditation question. You can explore it experientially.
Additionally, any of the glimpse practices can be
supplemented with a shift of awareness to see if
you can notice that which is aware of all things.

To notice the noticer, instead of looking outward, look toward the looker; notice that part of
you that is noticing. You can ask yourself, "Who
is aware?" At first you might identify a sense of
a person looking out at things or noticing your
experience, but then what is aware of that looker?
You might even look forward and then flip your
attention to the sense of being aware of what
you're looking at.

Really have fun with this practice, because
it's challenging and there's not a right way to do
it. Try not to get caught up in theories, but keep
returning to the experience. Be open to whatever
you find.

21 \ NATURAL AWARENESS MEDITATION
MARINATE AND REFRESH

The previous chapter discussed mental shifts we can make to move toward natural awareness. Another way to shift into natural awareness is through the glimpse practices scattered throughout the book. Once we have shifted into natural awareness, through whatever means, we have moved along the spectrum of awareness practices from classical mindfulness meditation into natural awareness meditation.

Now we can meditate with natural awareness in order to refine, deepen, and prolong the experience. Some people call this "abiding in natural awareness"; the teacher Loch Kelly calls it "marinating in natural awareness."[1] When you lose touch with natural awareness in the midst of the meditation, you can learn to "refresh." Natural awareness meditation depends on our ability to marinate and refresh.

Marinate

When you marinate chicken, you let it sit in the marinade (I prefer ginger, soy sauce, and olive oil) for a period of time (thirty minutes minimum) so that the seasonings soak into and infuse the meat. The longer the chicken marinates, the tastier it is. What does this cuisine analogy have to do with the mind? Well, as I have described, even a moment of natural awareness, like a little bit of marinade, can be impactful.

But when that moment is extended, the flavors of the natural awareness really come out, so to speak. In natural awareness meditation, we practice extending, abiding, and resting in natural awareness.

When we rest in natural awareness, we might notice qualities that are present, like joy or humor or some other facet of the diamond I spoke about in chapter 11. In that case, marinate. Keep letting those qualities unfold. Experience them; notice what is happening in your body and mind. But don't try too hard, because too much effort might pull you out of the experience. Anything can happen: The qualities may grow and intensify. Other qualities may arise. The original qualities may fade away.

Thoughts will enter and, like clouds in the sky, just move through us. We might find emotions coming and going. Sometimes when I do extended natural awareness meditation, I feel joy, then vulnerability, then poignancy, then hilarity. I ride the wave of whatever is happening.

But sometimes, as we're marinating, a particular thought or emotion gets a bit ornery and demands attention. This tends to rock the natural awareness. What is happening is we are getting caught in or identified with the thought or emotion, and that clinging or identification is disturbing our awareness. If the clinging or identification starts to outweigh the natural awareness, we may soon find ourselves lost in thought or emotion. But if we notice that we are lost, just the noticing may allow the thought or emotion to dissolve, like salt in water. And natural awareness may be invigorated—or not.

Refresh

When a website isn't loading properly or is acting funny in our web browser, we often hit the refresh button. Usually that resetting fixes the problem. We can do the same thing in natural awareness meditation.

Let's say that after some time resting or abiding in natural awareness, you realize you are spacing out or lost in thought and disconnected from natural awareness. You will recognize this in the same way that in classical mindfulness you often realize you have gotten distracted and are lost in thoughts. So you might verbally (but silently) say to yourself, "Refresh." This reminder can initiate a subtle kind of resetting, in which you realign yourself with the natural awareness, which is actually not too far away. A few seconds prior, you were resting your mind in this place of well-being. So there is a noticing that you are no longer abiding, a reminder to refresh, and then a reconnection in a mostly effortless way—as if you had gently pressed the refresh button on your browser. You may have to refresh dozens of times while abiding in natural awareness. This refresh is what prolongs and deepens your natural awareness meditation session.

Ultimately natural awareness may dissipate on its own. In fact, it usually does. And that's absolutely fine. If we tried to make it stay all the time, then we'd be clinging to natural awareness, which is missing the point. Please trust that the movement in and out of natural awareness from ordinary mind is as natural and as expected as ocean tides moving toward and away from the shore.

In the meantime, marinate, abide, rest in natural awareness when it arises, refresh when necessary, and see what happens. It can be quite tasty.

22 ◗ STRUCTURING YOUR NATURAL AWARENESS PRACTICE SESSION

When you're ready to experience moving along the spectrum of awareness practices from classical mindfulness meditation into natural awareness meditation, what would that practice session look like? Here is what I recommend.

After you've sat down and set your motivation, ask yourself, "What is my mind like now? And what is needed? And what am I drawn to today?" See if answers intuitively arise in response. You can either follow your inner guidance or continue with the next recommendations.

It is helpful to first take some time to stabilize your mind. Most people find stability and clarity by doing a focused awareness practice—such as a breath awareness practice—for, say, the first third of the meditation session.

From here, you may find that your mind is drawn to a flexible awareness practice, as I've described in chapter 19. This is a good intermediary step toward natural awareness practice, as you let go of your anchor and turn your attention to whatever object grabs it. You could spend the next third of your meditation here.

The final third would be natural awareness meditation. As you have already learned in chapter 20, you can shift into natural awareness by relaxing effort, by broadening your awareness, or by dropping the focus on objects (moving to objectless awareness). Another option is to employ one of the glimpse practices scattered throughout this book; I described how to do this in "How to Use the Glimpse Practices."

Once you have shifted into natural awareness, you can rest or marinate there for the remainder of the session, refreshing as needed (see chapter 21). However, don't feel boxed in here; feel free to go back to earlier parts of the meditation sequence as needed.

Alternatively, you may start with focused awareness meditation to stabilize your mind and then shift to natural awareness meditation at the halfway point. It's up to you. You will have to stay attuned to yourself and experiment a bit to find out what works for you, keeping in mind it might be different on different days. Staying responsive to your inner unfolding is what makes meditation practice interesting.

23 ❧ EYES WIDE OPEN

The first time I was introduced to natural awareness practices, the teacher said, "You've been meditating a long time, and you have been practicing how to open your awareness. You open to everything that's arising—body sensations, breath, sounds, thoughts, emotions. So why do you close your eyes when you meditate? You don't close your ears!" *He has a point*, I thought. But then I continued to meditate with closed eyes for another ten years.

Most classical mindfulness practitioners meditate with closed eyes, and although it's not a requirement for the practice, closed-eye meditation has a lot of benefits. It can reduce distractions in order to increase our ability to concentrate. Some people feel that the darkness is soothing and helps them connect more directly to their inner experience. From time to time, however, students report they have a sense of claustrophobia, experience discomfort, or are more distracted when they meditate with their eyes closed. Opening their eyes helps them feel safer or more present, and so for them I encourage open, downcast eyes and a soft gaze.

I would say the majority of classical mindfulness meditation practitioners keep their eyes closed, although there are some who practice with open, downcast eyes. At some point, when practicing natural awareness, I made the transition to open-eyed practice, and now, while I sometimes close my eyes in meditation, honestly, I'll never fully go back to it!

When teaching natural awareness practices, I recommend that students try open-eyed practice. At first it can feel awkward or disorienting, but with some time and practice, students often find it facilitates access to natural awareness. With open-eyed practice, our open visual field can create openness in our mind or a broadening of attention (one of the mental shifts into natural awareness I talked about earlier). However, if closing your eyes during natural awareness meditation is easier and more comfortable for you, it is fine to practice with your eyes closed.

Beginning eye-openers often report sandy- or dusty-feeling eyes, lots of blinking, or disorientation, and some decide to continue on with eyes closed. But those who stick with open-eyed meditation through the transition—by acknowledging and staying with the awkwardness while letting their eyes rest on the visual field—find it helps them access natural awareness.

Once open-eyed meditation is comfortable for you, I recommend going outside to a place with a beautiful view, such as the beach or a high hill, and simply looking. Settle back, open to the visual field, soften your belly, rest your mind, and receive the beauty. The nature itself may evoke natural awareness, as I talk about in chapter 53. Don't try too hard.

OPEN YOUR EYES

Opening our eyes while we meditate or opening our eyes in a relaxed, meditative way in daily life is a wonderful doorway into natural awareness.

To try this glimpse practice in meditation, when your mind feels stable, open your eyes. Let your eyes cast their gaze on whatever is in front of you. Look with awareness. Try not to get lost in the story, thinking about the visual object(s), but simply let your eyes rest on the visual field. Let your eyes be soft. Keep your belly soft.

In daily life, decide at any moment that you want to shift into an open-eyed, relaxed, broad viewing of whatever is in front of you. This practice may be slightly easier to do when the view is appealing. You can even try looking out the window at nature. Instead of being sucked into the stories, thoughts, and reactions to sights, as we usually are, settle back, soften your gaze, soften your belly, and simply look.

In both cases, see if you can let your peripheral sense dominate. Can you not only look at what is in front of you but also take in what is happening from multiple directions? How expansive can your visual field be?

Don't strain your eyes; try to keep them soft. If they feel tight or itchy or as if they are full of sand, just relax them or close them for a while, then open your eyes again if you wish to keep going with this practice.

Sense the impact of this practice on your awareness. What happens to thoughts when you rest with this visual field? Who is seeing?

24 ◗ MIX IT UP

Although the different practices on the spectrum of awareness can be done sequentially, most natural awareness practitioners tend to mix or alternate between different types of awareness practices, shifting between focused, flexible, and natural awareness.

A meditation session for me might go like this: I wake up in a bit of a sour mood. I sit down to meditate, and the first thing I notice is my resistance. I'm actually feeling a little sad, and this sadness seems big enough that I don't really want to practice. So I might place my hand over my heart, relax my posture, and send a bit of kindness to myself.

As I begin to notice warmth in my body, I can bring focused awareness to the sadness—feeling it, sensing it, maybe flexibly noticing the story or thoughts I have about it or maybe not. Then the sadness might soften a bit, and the warmth begins to pervade my whole body.

I check in to see if my mind is stable, calm, ready. I'm still a bit distracted, so I might try a little more focused awareness, using classical mindfulness meditation: I focus on my breathing in and out for a few minutes, allowing stability and calm to arise. Then I'll check in again, and perhaps I'll gently shift to a broader awareness—one that can include the remnants of the emotion, but in such a way that it has a transparency, that allows me to see through the emotion. It's not gone, but it's significantly thinner. I've already begun to touch into natural awareness.

Now I open to my back body (a glimpse practice that often works well for me). Then I expand my awareness further, and I notice my mind seems to have entered the territory of natural awareness: I feel expansive, relaxed, and really quite present. It's as if I couldn't be anything other than aware, and it feels very joyful.

After a few minutes of marinating here, refreshing a few times, I notice the thought *Oh no, I forgot to buy food for my daughter's lunch!* popping into my head. Perhaps the thought dissolves into the larger awareness, but if it doesn't, I might recognize it as thought, labeling it, feeling the underlying anxiety in my body, and breathing a bit to find some calm with it. (I've shifted back into classical mindfulness meditation.) If and when the thought no longer grabs me, I find an organic return to my natural awareness; spontaneously I feel relaxed, open, and once again fully present. I'm not focusing on any particular object. I feel simultaneously expanded yet within my own body. I remain there for the last five minutes of my session, refreshing when needed.

I might rest there, marinating in natural awareness, for some time, until my daughter shouts, "Mommy, I'm awake!" Time to stop meditating. I make a mental note to rummage for food for her lunch in the freezer. The day begins.

This is one example of a varied meditation practice session that includes natural awareness practice. Every session is entirely different, but it may give you a sense of how we can move in and out of different practices as they are called for. Developing this flexibility requires trusting your own practice experience and the ability to respond as needed in the midst of your meditation session.

25 ❧ TRUST THE HEALING

On many days I have sat down to meditate and been overtaken by an emotion. Anxiety, for instance, hits me hard in my gut. It may feel quite strong—so strong that I can barely meditate. I'd rather do anything else. And I have been known to call it a day and bury myself in a book or check my emails instead of face the emotion.

Experiencing emotions is a normal part of meditating. With both classical mindfulness and natural awareness meditation practices, emotions often surface, as if they are plants longing to grow toward the light. The light is awareness. Awareness (of any type) is very safe; a fully aware mind is completely safe—free of attachment and aversion. Our job is to recognize the fact that the grief or fear, pain or anger, or any other emotion is arising because that is the truth of the moment. With positive intentions as a baseline, we can trust the healing that comes as we shine the light of awareness on whatever emotion arises.

This space of safety is exactly where healing can occur. When we speak to a therapist or a trusted friend, finally able to get something off our chest as they fully listen to us with compassion, we experience a healing effect. Similarly, this healing can occur in natural awareness meditation (as well as in classical mindfulness). Why? Our own nonjudgmental, loving, open, and aware mind meets the strong emotion and offers it the safety to integrate and potentially resolve.

When my daughter is struggling with sadness or any other challenging emotion, my job as a parent is to hold her in a loving presence. I don't have to fix her emotion, give her advice, tell her not to be sad, or take the pain away. My job is simply to be there for her. This approach is analogous to what we do for ourselves when meditating with our emotions.

Often when we practice and emotions arise, if we let them pass through us, physical knots loosen, and we deepen into greater relaxation. As we let these things that need to be healed surface and move through us, as we hold these processes in awareness and kindness, we then have more and more access to natural awareness. It takes a lot of awareness to be able to hold something challenging. Once the challenging emotion has blown through us, what's left is the strong awareness.

When anxiety surfaces during my meditation, I often put my hand on my chest lovingly. I let myself sense the anxiety as it emerges organically. Sometimes I use other practices, like offering loving-kindness to myself or saying the incredibly useful phrases "It's okay" and "You will get through this." I let the anxiety emerge in a field of loving awareness, trusting that it needs to come forward, trusting that I am up to the task of allowing it to do so.

So if emotions arise during your meditation session, there is nothing wrong. They are a part of you that can reveal itself in the light of awareness. In chapters 26 and 27 I'll offer you some tools for working with these emotions.

However, please know that if an emotion arises that feels stronger than you can handle, you need to seek the appropriate therapeutic or spiritual support.

Most of us travel through life with heavy, bulky emotional baggage. To our great relief, with meditative practices and other healing modalities, we can shrink this baggage to carry-on size.

A MIRROR ANALOGY

After settling your mind a bit, read this analogy slowly and let the image sink in—not to dwell on it, but to see how it impacts your consciousness.

Imagine your mind is like a mirror, crystal clear, reflecting only what comes in front of it. No opinion, no clinging, no aversion—just pure reflection of reality exactly as it is. Rest your mind like a mirror that purely reflects what is right here in front of you.

26 🔖 DIFFICULT EMOTIONS
RAIN

In classical mindfulness meditation I teach a basic tool for working with difficult emotions. This tool can be used in natural awareness meditation as well. The tool is a simple acronym, RAIN: **r**ecognize, **a**llow, **i**nvestigate, and **n**ot *identify with (or* **n**onidentification). Michele McDonald, a senior teacher in the insight meditation tradition, developed this acronym, which is now widely used.

R stands for *recognize*. When we're having an emotion, can we put a label on it? What is it we're feeling? Sadness? Fear? Irritation? Confusion? The simple act of labeling the emotion has the effect of calming us down and giving a bit of perspective: "Aha, I'm lost in anxiety!"

A is the reminder to *allow* the emotion to be there. From the perspective of mindfulness, every emotion we have is okay; it is what is happening in the moment and an authentic expression of our humanness. What we do with the emotion is another story. Not acting out of it in unhealthy ways is key. So with RAIN, the invitation is to let the emotion be there, to allow it. It's okay; it's human. In that way, we reduce resistance around the emotion, which often makes it worse.

I means *investigate*—not to ruminate on the source of the emotion, but simply to explore what is actually happening in our bodies while we are in the midst of the emotion. All emotions have a physiological correlate. They are not abstract ideas; our bodies are responding in the midst of emotions. So "investigate" asks us to feel into our bodies: "Oh, there's tightness in my chest, constriction in my stomach. My face is hot . . ." We might also examine accompanying thoughts: "What am I thinking as this emotion arises?"

N is for *nonidentification*. After executing the first three steps, you will automatically have a measure of nonidentification, which means not taking it so personally. Usually we are caught in our emotions. But if we have recognized, allowed, and investigated them, we are no longer lost in that identification. We move from *my* emotion, in which we are foundering, to *the* emotion, which is simply passing through us. We get a bit of distance, a bit of space.

This RAIN practice is a systematic approach to working with emotions during meditation practice or in daily life. Even just one or two of the steps when needed in the course of your day may lead to a bit of relief from the overwhelm of an emotion.

27 | DIFFICULT EMOTIONS
SALT IN THE LAKE

Let's say you have a glass of water, and you dissolved a tablespoon of salt into it. The water is going to be pretty salty. I wouldn't recommend drinking it. However, if you were at a lake and poured the same tablespoon of salt into the lake, the salt would simply dissipate, leaving very little trace of itself.

This analogy can help us understand how to work with emotions, specifically in the midst of natural awareness meditation. When our mind is tight and contracted and we have an emotion, it can feel like the emotion subsumes our mind, takes over, just like the salt would fully infuse the glass of water. However, if our mind is wide open and spacious, the emotion can become just another aspect of experience, moving through us, not affecting the boundless, expansive nature of our awareness—just like the salt in the lake.

How does this work practically? If we can shift into natural awareness in the midst of a strong emotion and attempt to hold the emotion within our awareness while keeping the larger view, often it can feel like the emotion dissolves into awareness itself, like a little salt into a vast lake. It's like the field of awareness is so big that it's not disturbed by the challenging emotion.

Another Approach: Broadening Your Awareness
If natural awareness feels far off in the midst of a strong emotion, a more doable approach is to shift your attention to the

sounds around you. Another option is to open your eyes and notice or feel the space around you. In either case, see if you can stay aware, and possibly even spacious, while at the same time letting that emotion be there. I sometimes call this practice "casting a sidelong glance" at the difficult emotion. It's possible to have both expanded awareness and the difficult emotion simultaneously. Either of these approaches may allow you to soften and open; they do not necessarily invite you to rest in natural awareness, but they point you in that direction.

Let's try it now.

Sit comfortably, eyes open or closed, and connect with your inner experience. Take a few mindful breaths.

Now notice if there is some kind of emotion present. If there is not, can you recall a recent difficult emotion? (Don't pick the most challenging one you can think of; choose something more moderate.) Notice how you experience that emotion in your body—tense belly, tightness in your chest, heat in your face.

Now, even though the emotion is present, can you turn your attention to the sounds around you? After you notice the sounds for a minute or two, you can then become aware of the space around you; either feel it physically or open your eyes and look with a wide-open perspective. Take a few breaths and feel the sense of space.

Notice what happens to the challenging emotion as you shift your attention to these other focuses. Is it possible to feel spacious and open while casting a sidelong glance at your emotion? In other words, is it possible to feel the emotion too in the midst of the space?

Sometimes just expanding your attention enables you to start to feel fully present, aware even in the midst of the emotion. The emotion is part of your expanded awareness too; it can't possibly be separate.

LISTENING EXPANSION

Several of the glimpse practices invite us to broaden our attention in atypical ways. While having a broad awareness is not technically natural awareness, it often can evoke a more expansive and relaxed feeling that can ignite a fuller resting within natural awareness.

When you are settled, turn your attention to sound. Listen to the sounds around you as they come and go, without getting caught in a story about them. Just notice the changing sounds in the room or outside the room, as if you were listening to music.

Now begin to expand your listening. Listen out to the distance. What is the farthest away sound you can hear?

Let your attention open to the full array of sounds, near and far. Sustain this listening for a little while and notice how your mind feels as it expands as far as possible. Then rest with what you discover.

28 ❧ WHAT ABOUT THOUGHTS?

Most of us, most of the time, are lost in thoughts. We might call this *unfettered thinking*. We think and react and think some more and ruminate and worry and catastrophize and replay, and we don't have much awareness that we are thinking. This is what an untrained mind is like. We can train our mind to have a different relationship to thoughts. Classical mindfulness meditation and natural awareness meditation have different approaches to thinking (although the different approaches may sometimes overlap or be used in either type of meditation).

In one type of classical mindfulness meditation, focused awareness practice, in which we are trying to cultivate concentration, thoughts are considered distractions. We attend to a main focus (such as our breathing); when we notice we are distracted, we return to our main focus.

When we have more stability, thoughts don't have to be distractions. We can turn our attention to thoughts, noticing them as another object of meditation. We might even label them: *planning, remembering, imagining*. Labeling thoughts when they become predominant but then returning to our focus is flexible awareness practice. In flexible awareness practice, we can take it even further: noticing thought after thought after thought is flexible awareness of mental activity.

In natural awareness meditation, we have relaxed, broadened our attention, and dropped the objects of attention. Well, thoughts are objects. So in natural awareness meditation, we are not focusing on thoughts but are turning our attention to awareness itself, in the ways I have described throughout the book.

Experientially, it means that in natural awareness meditation, thoughts are present, generally, but they are usually in the background, in that we don't focus on them. They are arising in our awareness, but we are not in their grip, not clinging to them. We don't have to do anything about them. They often appear to be weightless or transparent. We can see through them. Because they are not our central focus, they may feel somewhat indistinct.

Sometimes in natural awareness meditation we may become naturally and effortlessly aware of thoughts. We may experience them, not as separate from our larger field of awareness, but as part of it. In this case, we can think from a naturally aware place. There are even times in natural awareness meditation when thoughts appear slower than usual, are very subtle, or are even almost nonexistent.

What typically happens for most people is that, at a certain point, our minds get caught again in thinking. A thought or memory or worry captures us. In that case, we have shifted out of resting in natural awareness. To return to natural awareness, we need to notice that thought and then refresh or "melt back" into natural awareness (see chapter 39).

29 ❧ CONCENTRATION AND NATURAL AWARENESS

In my meditation tradition, we sometimes use mindfulness practices to develop concentration. A concentrated mind is one that is stabilized, unified, focused, and collected. Because most people's minds are typically distracted, it is useful to spend time cultivating concentration—not for its own sake, but in the service of seeing clearly.

Here's a simple example: Did you ever, as a child, play with a magnifying glass, the sun, and a piece of paper? If you get it at the right angle, the magnifying glass can harness the sun's rays and can create a beam of light strong enough to burn the paper. This is similar to how our mind works. Most of the time our mind, like the sunlight, is scattered, but with some practice, we can focus our mind enough to create a laser-like awareness that has significant power. (Okay, maybe not laser-like, but certainly more focused.)

In classical mindfulness meditation, we can do a focused awareness practice of breath awareness for extended periods of time. We return to our breath when our attention is distracted away, and this practice can lead to a concentrated mind. In other meditation traditions, we might repeat a particular word or stare at a candle or an image. These tools function the same way.

Typically, once we have a concentrated mind, we can use the concentration for different types of practice, such as deepening our focused awareness, flexible awareness, or natural awareness.

It is my experience that having a concentrated mind is an excellent support to cultivating natural awareness. It is not absolutely necessary, but it is useful, especially for helping natural awareness stabilize—meaning occur for longer periods of time, with greater consistency, depth, or clarity.

Sometimes we can access natural awareness, and we don't seem to be concentrating. Natural awareness spontaneously appears in the midst of our day or surprises us when we sit down to meditate. If that's the case, just enjoy it! For the most part, however, you probably see that on days when your mind is scattered, it's often hard to let it rest in awareness. You keep obsessing about why your child is refusing to practice her musical instrument and why your bathroom sink keeps getting clogged (okay, maybe that's my mind!). Natural awareness can feel miles away.

On these very scattered meditation days, my suggestion is to just focus on your breathing for the majority of your session. Feel your breath in your abdomen, chest, or nose, moving in and out. When your mind wanders, bring it back to the breath. Then, toward the end of your session, stop concentrating or trying to do anything in particular and see what happens. You may find your mind spontaneously shifts into natural awareness.

Paradoxically, on those days when your mind feels tight or contracted, a more open awareness practice may be called for. You can try settling back and listening to sounds as they come and go. Expand even further: what's the farthest away sound you can hear?

Experiment, within your own practice, with the interplay of concentration and awareness.

30 ❧ ANXIETY
WHEN THERE'S NO GROUND

I remember one of the first times I opened into a strong experi-ence of resting in natural awareness. This was during one of my first long meditation retreats, and I suddenly I felt an absence of holding on tightly to anything—thoughts, emotions, even my sense of self. At first it felt very joyful and free, and then a few seconds later it felt terrifying and groundless. I opened my eyes and went in search of my teacher, who assured me the terror I felt was quite normal.

My case was extreme, but why might a practitioner occa-sionally encounter anxiety, fear, or discomfort in natural awareness practice?

One reason is that many of us are used to having an anchor in our meditation practice. As discussed in chapter 17, a med-itation anchor is something we can always return to, such as our breathing. When we switch to an objectless practice, we no longer have a concrete anchor to rely on, to provide a kind of safety, familiarity, and stability. In natural awareness practice, our anchor is awareness! Since awareness isn't tangible (like our breath or our body sensations), anchoring in awareness can create anxiety.

There's a simple fix: In the midst of open, objectless prac-tice, from time to time return to your anchor—your breath or even concrete body sensations. Focusing on something tan-gible helps most people feel a bit more grounded. It's even possible to have relaxed, open, spacious attention while still attending to your breath. Play with this practice a little and see if that is true for you.

Sit comfortably in a chair and close your eyes. After settling a bit, let your awareness open. Listen to the sounds around you, trying to hear faraway sounds. Notice your body and feel the expansion of awareness beyond your physical form, as if you could feel it 360 degrees.

Open your eyes if you wish and expand your vision, looking in a relaxed and wide-open way. As you're doing this, is it also possible to feel your body breathing? Can you notice the air moving through your nose or up and down in your belly or chest? Can you also feel your feet on the ground? Feel the stability of your feet touching the earth.

Continue holding this breath and body awareness simultaneously with noticing the expansion. It is possible to do both? What is the experience like?

Another reason we might feel anxiety in natural awareness practice is that strong emotions can surface as we're practicing, as discussed earlier. If you have a classical mindfulness practice, you probably have experienced this phenomenon. Anxiety may arise in your natural awareness practice when life is especially challenging or when you are worried about something. In that case, please work with it as you would with any emotion; you can refer to chapters 26 and 27 for guidance.

The third reason we might feel anxiety during this practice is that opening to natural awareness requires nonclinging, which is counter to what we normally do (cling!). Our minds are used to grasping at everything (including thoughts, emotions, opinions, experiences), trying to sustain them and make them "ours." Or we push things away when they appear disagreeable. This is another form of clinging that paradoxically manifests itself as what we call *aversion*—hating, disliking, fearing, or running away from an experience. In natural awareness practice, we merely rest our mind, not grasping after or pushing away anything, but letting the state of nonclinging occur, which deepens our awareness. As I experienced in my early meditation retreat, initially this state can feel scary, because it's unfamiliar.

See if you can stay with it. If you can let the anxiety arise as just part of the practice, as clouds in the sky of your mind, you may find that it subsides, and you may discover that the state of nonclinging is actually more soothing than the familiar and comfortable state of grasping after or pushing away everything.

One of my teachers, Joseph Goldstein, once shared this analogy: Imagine you are skydiving, jumping out of a plane, and you suddenly realize you don't have a parachute. I'm sure you would be terrified. Next, imagine that you look down, and there is no ground! I spent a number of years chewing over this metaphor (and so can you). But it indicates to me that even in the midst of profound letting go, it's an illusion there was something to hold on to in the first place. It's also an illusion that we are going to crash and burn. Perhaps there is no ground.

360-DEGREE BODY EXPANSION

This is another expansion practice that shifts us out of our forward focus and into other ways of knowing.

Get comfortable and take a few breaths. When you are ready, notice whatever physical sensations are obvious to you: tingling, itching, heaviness, lightness, movement, warmth—whatever. Can you notice these sensations simultaneously, or are they happening sequentially? Try to have a global body sense, aware of everything that's going on simultaneously. Make sure to include sensations along the back of your body as well as the front.

Now begin to expand your awareness out from your body, moving outward in all directions. Try to get a sense of the space around your body. Can you feel into it? Make sure you are feeling fully into the space 360 degrees around, above, and below your body. Allow that sense of expansion to go outward into the room and even beyond, as far as you can.

You can play with the awareness of outer expansion while also simultaneously sustaining inner body awareness. Awareness can feel unlimited. Stay with this sense of expansion for a while and see what happens.

31 ❧ SPACING OUT
WHO AM I KIDDING?

A major pitfall awaits the natural awareness practitioner: we can delude ourselves into thinking we're practicing when actually we're merely ruminating, thinking, or spacing out.

It is quite easy for our minds to enter territory that is similar to a natural awareness—masquerading as a natural awareness, even convincing us that it *is* a natural awareness—when it's really not. Because in natural awareness practice we are not trying to limit thoughts, it's hard to know if we are just spacing out and thinking or actually resting in natural awareness.

Sometimes we sit down to meditate, and our minds think. Our attention wanders off, worrying about the fact that *my car needs air in its tires, and it seems like they always need air, and maybe there's a puncture in one of them, and I should take my car to the mechanic to get the tires checked, and* . . . Although this sounds to you and me like thinking, it could be very easily construed as resting in awareness in the midst of thoughts. But resting in awareness in the midst of thoughts is actually a very different activity than unfettered thinking (which is what I was describing). When we are aware of thoughts, awareness is present; we know our mind is thinking. Here we simply think or space out, but delude ourselves into thinking our thinking isn't thinking or that our spacing out isn't spacing out!

I will admit I have spent many a meditation session thinking. I don't know anyone who hasn't. In fact, I have generated some of my best to-do lists during meditation. Am I proud of this? Not exactly. When we are lost in thought or spacing out, the simple remedy is to return to a present-moment experience, such as our breath or the touch of our feet on the floor or another physical sensation. This helps us reestablish mindfulness.

Sometimes, alas, there is thinking that is so subtle we barely notice it. This kind of thinking is so hard to identify, sometimes we realize only after the fact that we were lost in subtle thinking.

If you are wondering whether you are lost in thought or otherwise not in the midst of natural awareness practice, here are some questions to ask yourself:

- Does your mind feel crisply aware, or does it feel like it's in a fuzzy, "just kind of" awareness?

- Are thoughts coming and going, like clouds in the sky?

- Can you tune in to the field in which thoughts are arising (the sky)?

- Can you tell if you are even slightly caught in your thoughts?

- Are you having any reactivity to the thoughts, even subtly?

Even with such questions, you still may not be able to figure out whether you're lost in subtle thinking. It's not always easy to recognize what is going on in our minds. Unfortunately, there is no magic formula for identifying subtle thinking posing as natural awareness; each of us has to be kindly vigilant for self-deception.

32 ❧ BUSY MIND

There will be plenty of days when you sit down to meditate and your mind is out of control. Natural awareness seems impossibly far off. Just this morning I woke up, went over to my meditation chair, and began to think. I had a lot to think about: All the things I had to do today. All the emails I had to respond to and the list of calls I had to return. The fact that my daughter will need braces one day, and I still don't have an orthodontist. I even thought about how I'm supposed to be practicing awareness and all I can do is think about orthodontics and my to-do list.

Every now and then, amid this racing, hyperactive mind, I would have a moment of awareness—as if waking up from a dream. It was the moment I'd realize I was lost in thought; that's a moment of awareness. Perhaps it lasted only a breath or maybe even half a breath. And then I would sink back into the maelstrom.

Guess what? I'm normal. This is what the human mind does. We spend most of our lives busy and distracted. We can also speculate that the human brain has evolved to search for threats, to be constantly on the alert. When we sit down to meditate, our brain just does what it's always done. And we have the task of trying to calm this wild mind.

But having a busy mind is completely workable. First we need to remember that a busy, restless mind comes with the territory of (any type of) meditating—that it is not a problem. Then there are two tactics you can try:

- You can focus on your breath or another single
  object with renewed effort. Concentrating
  on a single object creates stability and focus
  in your mind. After a few minutes or a bit longer,
  your mind may settle.

- If concentrating feels hopeless, try the opposite:
  Let your mind get as spacious as possible. Let
  it run wild. Try to sense your body or listen to
  faraway sounds from time to time so you're not
  completely lost in thought. But otherwise just let
  your mind be. Broadening your awareness this way
  can have a calming and stabilizing effect.

I tried that second tactic, letting my mind become spacious,
one morning. And after a while (I can't tell you how long), I
noticed a quality of presence emerging from underneath the
busyness. I started to feel more "there." After a longer while, I
was really there. Sometimes it takes some patient waiting to let
your mind run itself into exhaustion, so to speak, and what's
left is more focus, concentration, and perhaps even some natural awareness.

THE SPACE BETWEEN THINGS

I talk often about shifting attention from objects to the awareness in which all objects are contained. We can get at this expansive concept by playing with the space between things.

While meditating with open eyes, shift into mindful seeing, softly gazing at what is in front of you and/or having an awareness of the periphery. Once you feel stably aware of the visual field, for fun, see if you can notice the space between the objects rather than the objects themselves. Don't focus on what your eyes are naturally drawn to, but instead on the space surrounding those things. Soften, relax, and connect with the space. What happens as you do this? Trust what emerges, letting whatever unfolds unfold. Relax and marinate in your discoveries.

In daily life you might try this glimpse practice outside under a night sky. Can you notice the space in between the billions of stars?

33 ❧ SLEEPY TIME

On some days our meditation practice can provide an excellent source of much needed sleep. This is nothing to worry about. Most of us in the United States do not get enough sleep, trying to get by on five or six hours when we need a minimum of eight, as the sleep scientists tell us.

So when a sleep-deprived person sits comfortably, perhaps closes their eyes, and tries to meditate, what tends to happen is a recipe for napping, not awareness. In fact, today I spent a nourishing hour of meditation completely asleep. Every now and then I would realize this and, with great will, lift my bobbing head up. But soon it would go back down, and I would be sound asleep again.

Sometimes we don't actually fall asleep but exist in a kind of dreamy presleep state. Or we feel like we're floating around, not really anchored to anything, not so aware, but not actually asleep. There are many meditative states that are close to sleepiness, so it's easy to get them confused. The test is whether or not there is awareness present. If not, it's likely you were asleep, which may have made you feel quite peaceful, but not so aware. Sometimes we can feel like we're resting in natural awareness when we're actually dreamy, spacey, or sleepy.

What do we do? Most importantly, don't make it into a problem. Try to practice at a time of day when you are least likely to get sleepy. If you do notice sleepiness occurring, open your eyes and stand up. Take a break.

Or take a nap and try again later; it's possible that you just needed sleep. Years ago my great-aunt, who was in her eighties, would attend my mindfulness classes at UCLA. She was struggling with insomnia. She later informed me she got the best sleep of the week in my classes. I thought that was a great success.

Awareness can be present even in sleepiness. To determine if it is, here's what you can look for:

- You can notice what sleepiness feels like in your body, practicing a deliberate mindfulness of the state of sleepiness and your reaction to it. (Aversion, anyone?)

- You can try to tap into an underlying sense of awareness that is present even while you are sleepy.

We can notice, be curious about, and connect with awareness no matter what the circumstances are—including being sleepy. That is the beauty of awareness. It doesn't require life to be a certain way in order for it to be present. Awareness is always present. Just tap into it, even in the midst of the sleepiest mind experience.

(I know you are going to ask, "Is awareness present when you are asleep?" Honestly, I can't answer that question.)

34 ❧ SUBTLE SLEEPINESS OR DULLNESS

As I mentioned in the previous chapter, getting some sleep during meditation is not a bad thing! But it is not practicing awareness. What is confusing is when we are in dreamy, peaceful states that are subtler than outright exhaustion or falling asleep and we wonder, "Is this natural awareness?"

It is a tricky question to answer because a peaceful, concentrated mind and a sleepy mind are very close experientially. In fact, if we have a lot of concentration but not much energy, we might find ourselves getting sleepy. (The reverse would be a lot of energy but not much concentration, which makes us restless.) A concentrated mind can feel very enjoyable, but without the energy to bolster it, it has a sinking or sometimes dull quality to it.

So people often report having a very peaceful mind with not much happening, and they think this is a kind of natural awareness. Or their mind seems very subdued, quite peaceful, but it has a dull quality to it. In other words, there is no brightness—no cognizing or awareness, just peace and a bit of disconnection. Some people report a mind that seems not so present, yet this state feels great.

To determine whether you're truly in natural awareness or just in a subdued, peaceful state, while meditating you can ask these two questions:

- Is awareness present? If not, pay closer attention to exactly what it is you're experiencing in your body and mind. As we bring curiosity to it, we can sometimes increase the energy and bring in more awareness, which counteracts the dullness.

• Is clinging present? Are you, for example, subtly enjoying the dulled-out state? As we investigate here, we might discover subtle clinging, and by shining the light of awareness on it, the clinging lets go.

Again, it's not always easy to tell whether you are experiencing subtle sleepiness or natural awareness, but these two questions will help you if you are not sure.

EXPAND EVERYTHING

This practice brings together all the previous glimpse practices that involve the expansion of awareness. Remember, we usually focus our attention forward and narrowly. By opening to a more expansive perspective, we can sometimes find ourselves accessing natural awareness.

Get comfortable and close your eyes. Begin with expanded listening—listening out to the far reaches of your hearing. Once you've expanded your listening, open your eyes and broaden your vision. Let your field of vision be expansive, noticing the space between things and viewing peripherally. Then expand your body awareness. First notice your back body. Then begin to expand further out, sensing the field around, above, and below you in 360 degrees.

At this point, your senses of hearing, sight, and feeling should all be expanded. From here, you can begin to play with that expansion. Can you stay expanded but also feel embodied? Can you have simultaneous inner and outer awareness? What predominates?

When you notice yourself tensing, just relax your body. It might be possible to stay connected to only one field (sight, sound, feeling), or perhaps you can feel them all simultaneously. Be curious and know that you can't do this expansion practice wrong.

Also notice: Who is being aware? Can you sense the awareness that is knowing the expansion?

35 \ EMBODIMENT
DON'T GET CAUGHT IN THE HEAD

In the story "A Painful Case," James Joyce writes of the main character, "He lived at a little distance from his body."[1] This telling quote reminds us how common it is to live in a disembodied way. And I would speculate that since so many of us spend much of our days on computers and other electronic devices, the disembodiment is becoming even more commonplace.

Unsurprisingly, it's also a trap we can run into when practicing natural awareness meditation. We end up getting caught in the head, so to speak. As we're already a bit disconnected from our bodies and used to attending to life with a forward focus, it would make sense that natural awareness would be a field of awareness right in front of us. Moreover, since most people associate consciousness with their brains and sense organs, we assume awareness is in our heads.

When people access natural awareness, they typically experience natural awareness as *only* right in front of them. There is nothing wrong with this experience per se, but it is incomplete. Natural awareness is actually directionless. It can be externally experienced in a forward-facing direction, but it can also be experienced in all directions—behind, above, and below us.

Additionally, we can experience it internally, when we include our bodies in our natural awareness. All of the qualities we might notice in forward, external natural awareness can be present inside our very body. We might feel spacious, soft, warm, relaxed, and any of the other facets of the diamond I talked about in chapter 11. Any of these qualities could be sensed quite strongly inside our bodies. Then we can make another step and sense natural awareness externally and internally simultaneously.

It's an important shift for the awareness to become sensed internally, or *embodied*, because this shift allows us to *function* from the natural awareness. Natural awareness starts to feel more like an aspect of our physical body, not just an aspect of our mind. We can lead our lives from a place of embodied natural awareness, in which we are not merely a head with a body dangling from it.

The next time you practice, see if you have fallen into this trap of experiencing natural awareness as only in your mind or outside of your body; sink your attention into your body while sustaining the natural awareness externally and see what happens. Is it possible to have both types of awareness simultaneously?

When practitioners shift into natural awareness, they may immediately begin to worry they're going to lose that awareness. Subtle, or even not-so-subtle, anxiety is created. Or, worse, they rest their mind in natural awareness for a while, and when it starts to fade, they think something is wrong with them because they can't make it stay. So they start manipulating their experience to sustain it: *Quick, try another glimpse practice! I know that one worked yesterday! Refresh! Refresh!*

Or they don't have access at any given moment to natural awareness, and feeling like something is wrong with them, they start pushing it, trying to make natural awareness happen. (By the way, that "they" I am writing about possibly may have been me at one point or another.)

All of these responses are natural and human. When experiences are enjoyable or beneficial, we want them to stay. When they are challenging or unpleasant, we want them to leave. Many meditation students struggle with learning how to relax a bit and allow meditation experiences to be there without grasping at them. When natural awareness arises, it is just a meditation experience. Yes, it's a profound and lovely one, but it too will change and pass, just like anything else.

If natural awareness has not arisen and you feel yourself longing for it, then drop in a few glimpse practices in a relaxed manner, trying to minimize your expectations. If that doesn't work, please don't beat yourself up. Just acknowledge the truth of things as they are: ordinary mind is present. Don't keep pushing, trying to make "it" happen. Soften and relax into the absence, as this relaxation, in and of itself, is a kind of freedom.

If natural awareness does arise but feels tenuous and fleeting, try a few glimpse practices you know work for you. Try to refresh. If you're still finding it out of your reach, forgive yourself and be with what *is* here.

Don't force things. Let natural awareness stay as long as it stays. Sometimes our ordinary mind hijacks us, we forget about natural awareness, and we head out the door into the busyness of our day. Other times, natural awareness fades, and we feel the loss of it or long for it since it is often so lovely. Just notice these emotions arising; it's okay. You can try again later.

Natural awareness has a life of its own, based on the accumulation of your practice. It will arise and sustain at different times in your life and throughout your lifetime of practice. Natural awareness is not a constant thing; it is not an "it" that you can make happen. Learn to surf the waves and let go into the radical nature of what is.

37 ◗ DROP THE BANANA

In Thailand, here's how hunters capture monkeys: They hollow out a coconut through a small hole about the size of a monkey's hand when it is outstretched. They then put a banana inside the coconut hole and leave the rigged coconut outside in the jungle, secured to the tree.

When the monkey comes upon the coconut, he reaches in and makes a fist around the banana. But then he can't pull his hand out because he can't remove his fist from the small opening. The monkey is caught. There's one simple solution that doesn't usually occur to our poor trapped monkey: drop the banana. Sadly, the monkey would let himself be captured rather than release the coveted banana.

I know, it's a terrible story about monkey hunting, but it's a helpful analogy for how the human mind works. We are often captured by our desires or by a multitude of emotions, thoughts, opinions, and so on. We can find freedom by letting go, but most of us tend to stay captured. When we are caught, our task is to drop the banana—to drop whatever we're hanging onto. As painful as it is, letting go is the only way to find freedom.

The key to dropping the banana is awareness: knowing we are caught and then using our awareness to relax the grip on whatever it is that is holding us in bondage. And I might argue that when we relax, what is it we might possibly open to? Natural awareness.

ASK YOURSELF . . .

Here's another question to ask yourself to help you access natural awareness. This is not an analytical question but is meant to help you listen deeply inside yourself.

Once you have a bit of concentration in meditation, or at any point in the day, drop the following question into your mind:

. "What is here in the wake of letting go?"

38 ◊ CAUGHT OR FREE?

One could say there are two modes of being: caught and free. What I mean is that much of the time we are caught in our thoughts and emotions, grasping the banana, believing thoughts to be real, creating loops of suffering as we career from thoughts to emotions and back again. Sometimes they don't cause suffering per se, but our thoughts keep us glued to our fears, desires, opinions, assumptions, self-righteousness, or whatever is the flavor of the hour.

If we're not caught—and we're not distracting ourselves—we might possibly be free. "Free" meaning, well, simply, not lost in a maelstrom of thinking and feeling in a way that causes suffering. We've dropped the banana. Generally, when we feel free, there is a sense of relief in our minds, like we've let go of a heavy burden. This freedom is most easy to experience in the moments when we truly let go.

Here's a simple example: You want a cookie. You've already had ten cookies today. You know you don't really need another one, yet it feels like your life depends on it. To work with this desire, feel into it for a moment with mindfulness: "Gosh, my stomach is clenched. I'm salivating. My face is hot." Then realize, "Okay, it's just a feeling, nothing more," and your mind may drop it: "I don't need to satisfy the desire right now." Then what's left? Possibly a feeling of freedom, of peace, of relief.

We can learn to live more and more in that place of letting go. Awareness of any type is tremendously helpful for showing us when we are caught, and *seeing we are caught is what allows our minds to let go*. We don't let go out of willpower necessarily, although sometimes that's what it takes, but actually out of clear seeing.

Now, this process of getting caught and being free is happening all the time. It happens not just with cookies or other goodies we want; we also get lost in our thoughts, emotions, and opinions—caught in believing them—on a moment-to-moment basis.

When we begin to meditate, we may first discover that all we're doing is getting lost in thought, with a moment of respite here and there as we find our breath again. But over time and with experience, we start to have more and more moments of being free. Through the clear seeing of awareness, our mind lets go. In both classical mindfulness and natural awareness meditation, we notice that our mind is hooked, and then we settle back into a place of ease and letting go. We train our mind to recognize that *the letting go feels better than the being caught*. How relieving and joyful!

Then over time, throughout our day, we regularly check in to our minds and notice whether we are caught or free. And if we're caught, we soften into our being, relax, unclench our belly, and let go. We often experience a rush of quiet peace and ease that begins more and more to feel like home.

Once many years ago, while practicing with one of my teachers, I asked a question: "How do you make natural awareness increase?" His response was, "Natural awareness doesn't increase. Clinging lessens." I have been chewing on this particular comment for about twenty years, but I think you can see in it the direct relationship between letting go and natural awareness.

39 ❧ HOOKED? MELT BACK

Melting back is what I call the moment of moving from being identified with, hooked, caught, or lost in our thoughts (or emotions or stories or dramas) to settling back into natural awareness. We drop the banana, as discussed in chapter 37. Often we experience a profound sense of relief, as if coming home or returning to ourselves. Whenever we are caught, we rigidify, clench our belly, or tighten our body in some other way. Melting back feels to me like the movement from being rigid, tight, forward facing, outer directed, and congealed or hardened to being settled back or soft. It is almost like ice melting—or, better yet, like chocolate melting. Can you imagine what that feels like?

Here's how it looks in natural awareness meditation (although you may find a similar process in classical mindfulness meditation): At any point in your meditation, you notice that your mind is hooked; it is lost in a story (or a thought or an emotion or something else), and it feels tight, contracted. Sometimes merely the recognition that you're caught allows you to melt back into awareness. You soften your body, soften your mind, and a simple letting go occurs. Natural awareness rushes in, and you often feel peace or relief or even a sense of freedom. *What is here in the wake of letting go?*

You might find yourself having a meditation session in which you go in and out of being caught and being free. You notice you're entrapped, and then you melt back into resting in natural awareness. And then you're hooked again, and you melt again. It's actually a wonderful dance—going back and forth between the two.

This dance can also happen in daily life. You're at a stoplight, and you realize you are anxious about making your appointment on time. Then you realize you are caught or hardened, and in that mere recognition, your body softens, and you melt back. What peace!

Sometimes the awareness that you're caught or hardened isn't enough, and melting back takes a gentle reminder—a label or a few mental words like *let go* or *it's okay*. Sometimes it takes a deliberate softening of your body, and as your body softens, your mind lets go. Sometimes if you turn your attention to whatever physical sensations you are feeling (such as tightness in your throat), simply allowing it to be there rather than resisting it, melting back can occur as well.

Sometimes you recognize you are hooked, and despite your best intentions to melt back or let go or drop the banana, you're simply hooked. Please remember, being hooked is completely normal! We'll address being caught in chapter 63.

MELTING BACK LIKE CHOCOLATE

When we notice we are rigidly caught in our drama, we can try this glimpse practice in which we soften, or "melt back," just like chocolate melts when heated.

Briefly sense into your body. Do you notice any areas of tightness? Check your belly, your ribs, your hands, your face and jaw. Now soften any part you noticed that felt tight. Think about hardened chocolate that's beginning to melt, if that analogy is helpful. Soften your facial muscles. Unclench your belly.

Notice if you are caught in a particular thought. Sometimes when we're hooked by a thought we have corresponding physical tightness. Did softening your body and melting back, just now, help to release the thought?

What happens to your mind as you melt back and release contractions? Feel into the soft, melty quality of your body and mind.

When you're finished, go get a piece of chocolate.

40 ❧ DOUBT

IS THIS IT?

Doubt is a pernicious obstacle because it can paralyze us and waylay our practice. Doubtful thoughts can feel very real, and we can question the foundation of our practice, thinking that our questions are good common sense. The biggest area of doubt I identify with natural awareness practitioners are the perennial questions "Is what I'm experiencing natural awareness, or is it something else? And how do I know?"

If you are uncertain, it is helpful to review the pitfalls we just talked about in chapters 31 through 36 to see if you've fallen into any of the obvious traps, such as spacing out, busy mind, sleepiness, dullness, or a "misbehaving" mind. Those chapters offer tools to help you make adjustments and shift back into natural awareness.

An immediate, subtle adjustment we can make is to notice if our mind is clinging in any way to anything. Our mind may be clinging, but we're not exactly sure where. Is there slight aversion, minute impatience, desire for another experience, resistance? These are all clinging states to look for. (Softening our belly also helps; scanning for tightness in our body is a good strategy for helping identify when we are clinging.) When we can see and name the clinging, *the state may let go of us*. (And I mean *may*. We can't make it let go.) And we can relax more into beingness.

Signposts

The truth is, unless you are working with a very advanced master who thoroughly knows the nuances of natural awareness practice and can even intuit in some way what's going on in your mind, you will never truly know whether you're experiencing authentic natural awareness or a similar, only subtly different, state of nonawareness.

You can, however, take your own word for it.

Ultimately, natural awareness is a subjective experience. Here are some signposts you can look for:

- Is clear perceiving happening?

- Are thoughts happening on their own, or are you caught in them?

- Is your effort relaxed, or are you trying to make something happen?

- Are you aware of the space that contains your present moment experience?

- Are you aware of awareness itself?

- How spacious does your mind feel?

- Does it feel like everything is happening on its own?

- Do you sense the awareness both internally (in your body) and externally (outside your body)?

- Are there qualities of well-being present, like luminosity, joy, humor, or ease, whether they are subtle or strong? (See chapter 11 for additional qualities of well-being.)

- Is there a part of you that simply knows you are resting in natural awareness? Sometimes for me, a voice says, "Ah, I'm here."

Use these signposts as questions to help you investigate the presence or absence of natural awareness. They are suggestions and describe different, sometimes contradictory ways students experience natural awareness. Please keep in mind that experiencing just one of these signposts is enough. They don't all have to be present simultaneously.

Most practitioners, over time, arrive at what they assume to be natural awareness for *them*, and each person's ways of experiencing it are different. You have to listen to that part of you that knows and *trust that* your *experience of natural awareness is on target*. Let that trust ripen and develop. Let it become the touchstone to which you always return—meaning that once you've had an experience of natural awareness that seems most like what I've described throughout the book, you can use that experience as a reference point for additional experiences. It may take a while to feel confident about this reference point, so be patient. And don't forget to continue to refine your understanding through ongoing practice, study, and outside guidance.

41 ◣ CLOUDS AND THE SKY

Here's an analogy that can help us access natural awareness: Our mind is like the sky—vast, open, spacious, transparent, and boundless. All our thoughts and emotions are like clouds that are passing across the sky. Sometimes they are light and wispy; sometimes they are heavy and stormy. For most of us, the heavy clouds seem to obscure the sky-like nature of our mind. Our job is to find our way back to the sky, letting the thoughts be there without making them a problem or losing touch with our awareness.

Here's why we get so easily lost in the clouds: We *identify* with those emotions and thoughts, thinking they've obscured our sky. This means we get caught in them, believing them to be true, real, the only reality. We get lost in the clouds of self-judgment, anxiety, grief, rage, comparison, worry, and so on. We get so identified that we forget the sky.

Thoughts do have objective reality, but they are merely thoughts. Clouds are *part* of the sky—part of our field of awareness. When we recognize how we've become identified with the clouds and release the identification, that nonclinging helps us reconnect with our natural awareness. We can return to the sky and see the thoughts as clouds passing by, part of the sky-like nature of our mind.

So when I'm meditating and I feel utter boredom, and that utter boredom seems unendurable, and the last thing I want to do is rest my mind (or meditate at all, for that matter), I am strongly identified with the boredom. I am not recognizing that it is merely a cloud passing by. Sometimes I remind myself of the sky-and-clouds analogy and try to see the boredom (or anything else I'm caught in) as a kind of cloud. I don't necessarily visualize it that way (although that visualization might spontaneously occur); the analogy is mostly an internal reminder that helps me shift perspective. If and when I can drop the identification, connecting with the sky, not the clouds, and let go of my belief in the boredom, I can often find a way back to natural awareness—to resting in the vast, open, sky-like nature of my mind.

MIND LIKE THE SKY ANALOGY

This is an invocation of an analogy. Read it slowly and let the image sink in—not to dwell on it, but to see how the analogy impacts your consciousness. Take in the analogy as you settle into your own sense of being. Or keep it in the back of your mind throughout a meditation session or during the day.

Imagine your mind is like the sky—wide open, spacious, boundless, endless, transparent. Everything that you encounter—thoughts, emotions, sensations, memories, sounds, images—is just like clouds floating by. Stormy clouds, wispy clouds—nothing can disturb the vastness of the sky. Settle back into the sky-like nature of your mind.

42 🔖 SELF-JUDGMENT
THE TYRANNY OF DOING IT RIGHT

One of the benefits of expanding our meditation practice along the spectrum of awareness practices to include natural awareness practice is the way this expansion can impact our sense of striving and the accompanying judgments.

When I was practicing classical mindfulness meditation in a monastery during my yearlong meditation retreat, I was, in my own mind, seldom good enough. There are ways we can practice meditation in which the effort emerges from a wholehearted desire to have more freedom. We strive, but we strive in a balanced way because of our passion for waking up. We strive because we know that it does take effort to rein in our wild minds and that with persistence we will see the fruits of practice: insight, clarity, and peace.

However, for me it was a little different. I believe I had all those healthy motivations, but I was also motivated by a very strong sense that I wasn't good enough—that if I didn't "get my A in meditation," somehow I was a failure. This led to more striving—and imbalanced striving at that. I started sleeping sitting up, thinking it would help me progress more quickly in my meditation. I had read that the great yogis in history had slept this way, so I thought perhaps that would speed things up for me. I would sit in my cross-legged meditation posture until I grew so exhausted that I would just pass out. When I awoke a few hours later, I would find my face against the floor, my body curled up in a ball under my mosquito net.

As I explained in the introduction, so much of my striving came from my own inner critic, who was never satisfied with me. If I could just attain some special state, then maybe I would be a worthy person. It was only by my falling apart that this motivation was revealed to me.

I have met many meditation students with similar stories. We try so hard to progress in meditation that we tie ourselves up in knots, often subverting the very thing we are aiming for.

Natural awareness practice was a balm for me because at its core is the understanding that we are already fundamentally whole. That awareness has always been present, that our mind's nature is to know, and that all we have to do is tap into this existing radiant presence.

When I present the possibility of not working so hard in meditation to students, I am often met first with disbelief. But once they try it, they experience a tremendous sense of relief and of pressure lifting. Many whose classical mindfulness practice had always been accompanied by self-critical voices saying, "Get back to the breath! Now!" or "Wow, you're a terrible meditator!" have reported those voices are relieved when they are practicing natural awareness meditation.

This isn't to say we shouldn't ever make an effort in meditation. We need to try to even not try! But our effort must be balanced. Natural awareness practice serves as a corrective for those who have gone too far in the effortful direction, resulting in a buildup of self-hatred.

I know for myself that, for the most part these days, my natural awareness practice feels infused with self-love. One of the most nourishing things I can do for myself is connect with the kindness and love, caring and compassion for myself that are woven into my natural awareness.

43 ❧ INNER GOODNESS

Are human beings fundamentally evil or good? Philosophers have been debating this question for centuries, and it's been explored in the context of evolutionary biology, psychology, religion, and other fields. I don't think there is any resolution on this one, and there probably never will be. A thorough discussion is beyond the scope of this book.

I fall in the camp of goodness. It's what I want to believe and how I want to live my life. I assume that everyone is fundamentally good. The obvious question is: But what about all the evil around us? The world is filled with examples of greed, hatred, violence, and misery. Well, I believe that the goodness inside us gets warped, distorted, and obscured. Due to trauma, strong conditioning, ignorance, or possibly severe personality disorders (in the case of sociopaths, for example), our inner goodness loses traction.

For many years I have been teaching about inner goodness: that we all have at our heart a goodness that is unimaginable. We have the capacity to love and be generous and kind and compassionate, because that is who we really are. We may be disconnected from our goodness, or it may be obscured, but it's always in there waiting to be uncovered.

Natural awareness practices are oriented from that place of inner goodness. Natural awareness is benevolent. It is permeated with qualities and connected to outcomes of compassion and joy and wisdom and peace. So when we tap into our natural awareness, we begin to find an ability to trust that goodness is fundamental to who we are, and ultimately we can grow to love ourselves.

We are not our anxiety; we are not our greed; we are not our self-judgments; we are not our rage. We are so much more than that. When we rest our mind in natural awareness, we let go of clinging, and we open to our innate goodness. First we experience this goodness in tiny, fleeting moments. Over time we actually start to believe in our goodness, and our life becomes its expression. Not that you won't fall back into self-judgment from time to time, but your natural awareness is always out there waiting for you, a growing whisper, calling your name.

ASK YOURSELF . . .

Settle your mind, relax, and pause. When you are ready, drop the following question into your mind. Listen deeply and see what emerges.

"What would be here if nothing were wrong?"

44 ❧ HOW COMPASSION FITS IN

Compassion is the genuine desire to alleviate suffering. It is often connected to action, although it originates as a feeling and an impulse. In world religions and spiritual traditions, compassion can be cultivated through specific meditation practices, prayers, or adherence to teachings. I've noticed that compassion tends to spontaneously arrive in conjunction with natural awareness. Let's see why this is the case.

As we practice letting go and resting our mind without agenda in a deeply relaxed and open state, as we recognize our own luminous awareness, we see that this awareness has certain qualities, one of which is compassion.

Compassion is inherent in natural awareness because natural awareness is connected to nonclinging. The less we identify with our dramas, the less we hold on to our sense of self-importance, and the more compassion shows up quite effortlessly and naturally. Rather than trying to preserve ourselves or build ourselves up, instead we make ourselves available to the world. People often experience a sense of interconnection—nonseparation from others or the world around us—during natural awareness practice. This connected feeling generates a compassionate response, as empathy arises from encounters with the thought of or actual contact with others' suffering. Compassion sometimes appears to be threaded through the natural awareness.

I've heard one teacher explain how compassion and action are embedded in each other. She says that the sun doesn't think,

"How can I help make plants grow?" It just offers its rays out to the world. That is its function. Compassionate response in natural awareness is a bit like that.

Moderate or intense feelings of compassion may arise spontaneously while we are practicing. Sometimes we feel as if we are holding the suffering of the whole world, yet our heart is responding and can contain it. Rather than experiencing pity, where we are overwhelmed by the suffering, we find that our heart is authentically moved to alleviate the suffering.

While natural awareness practice may seem like a practice of the mind, it is actually deeply connected to our heart. At times in natural awareness meditation we may find our attention naturally drawn to our heart. At other times we can deliberately turn our attention there and attempt to practice natural awareness, not from our head, but from our heart. We can imagine dropping the seat of awareness into our heart and becoming aware not only of what we feel internally but also of what we can sense externally (through sight, sound, and touch). It's a very interesting way to practice accessing natural awareness. We can then explore letting the positive emotions radiate out through our heart and into the world in all directions.

45 ❧ INTEND COMPASSION

In chapter 16 I spoke about clarifying motivations, setting intentions, and offering commitments as part of our meditation practice.

Every morning when I meditate, I say a short meditative prayer to begin my practice. It is of Buddhist origin, taken from Shantideva, an eighth-century Buddhist monk and scholar. It goes like this:

> For as long as space exists and sentient beings endure,
> May I be the living ground of love for all beings.

This intention has been part of my practice for as long as I can remember, and although I've probably said it thousands of times, it still moves me every time I recite it.

I say these words because my practice is connected to my love for the world. I say them because every time I do, I am reminded that my practice is connected intimately with the suffering of the world and is not about navel-gazing. I say them because they connect me to my deepest intentions for a life well lived: waking up and then being available for others.

So I open myself up to these words of compassion, and out of that, well, life takes its course. As I practice classical mindfulness and natural awareness, I find my self-centeredness reducing and a natural urge to serve arising and becoming the center of my life. While I'm not working in social service or involved in much activism these days, my life centers on helping individuals transform and seeding the effects into larger cultural and institutional change.

And as I look at my life over time, my intention is slowly manifesting itself. Whether I'm successful or not, I probably will never know. But each step of my day-to-day life feels right, and I can trust that.

HEART AWARENESS

In Western culture, people tend to assume our mind is located in our brain. However, in many other cultures the mind is considered to be situated in the heart area—located in the center of the chest, not in the physical heart.

This practice is a thought experiment, so have fun with it rather than trying to figure it out analytically.

After you are settled, drop your awareness down from your head into your heart area, and first feel what is present in your heart. Then imagine your heart is that which is sensing, seeing, hearing, perceiving, and feeling. To help you to do this, you can repeat a few times, "Drop the knowing into my heart."

What happens? Try looking through your heart, then hearing, then feeling, then knowing—all through your heart. Can your heart sense both inside of you and outside of you? Notice the emotional tenor to this way of practicing.

If feelings of love or compassion arise, you can bring in some basic well-wishing words to help diffuse the feelings, such as "May you be happy and peaceful. May you be at ease." Direct these words to whomever you feel drawn. If you feel kindness or compassion, allow it to expand throughout your body. If you don't, you can always say, "For whatever it is I'm feeling right now, may I hold this in kindness." Marinate in this heart-based knowing and see what happens.

46 ◗ RETREATS

We can jump-start or greatly support our daily meditation practice by participating in meditation retreats. I have spent many months and years in silent meditation retreats in retreat centers and monasteries in Asia and the United States. I love meditation retreats. If you haven't attended one and you have the means to take a few days or weeks out of your life, I encourage you to give it a try.[1]

A silent retreat in my tradition typically involves a structured schedule of alternating sitting and walking meditations, along with teacher guidance, dialogue, and hopefully some access to nature. All your meals are taken care of, usually, and you don't have anything to do except attend the meditation sessions and perform a work meditation (like washing pots) to help the retreat center function smoothly.

Why are retreats so valuable? For many reasons: First, they take us out of our typical routines so we don't have to employ the busy, responsible, to-do-list-checking, worrying, planning, taking-care-of-life mind. For me, the moment I step into a retreat center, I relax. I don't have to do anything except meditate, and with that recognition comes a freedom in my psyche that allows me to devote myself fully to the practice.

Second, it allows us to practice for extended periods of time. When we meditate daily (or dailyish) at home, we often do so for short periods. Although meditating for even a few minutes every day is valuable, when we have an extended period of practice, our concentration builds, and, as I talked about earlier, our minds have the chance to stabilize. Meditating for longer periods also allows for a depth of experience and insight to occur. When we are in the midst of our daily life and our ordinary concerns, we don't usually have the time to sustain our attention and cultivate a robust awareness.

The sheer number of hours spent meditating on retreat allows our concentration to build, and then we find our capacity to be aware strengthens. This stronger awareness, in turn, can allow a healing process to happen, as we have the space and time for emotions to move through us. We can get perspective on our personal challenges when we bring awareness and compassion to them. We also may find insights about the world arising from this concentrated mind. All of this understanding needs time and continuity of practice to develop.

Throughout this book I have shared how natural awareness can ripen over time: our awareness intensifies, prolongs, and becomes stronger and more refined at the same time. In longer retreats we can often find ourselves living in a natural awareness state for hours or days. We likely flow in and out of it, but the possibility of being in it is always present. So the extended periods offered by retreats are quite valuable.

But retreats can also be quite hard, and most people who haven't been on one are usually afraid to try it. Many people have told me flat out that they don't think they can do it. This apprehension is very common and quite natural, and I would encourage you not to let it get in your way. Those same people almost always describe their first retreat as being one of the most important things they have ever done in their lives, in spite of it being hard. Sometimes we meet our demons on retreats (loneliness, restlessness, fear, life challenges, and so on), but with teacher support and the skills of meditation, we can also contact internal resources we never knew we had.

ABC News anchor Dan Harris said after his first retreat, "It was the longest, most exquisite high of my life, but the hangover came first."[2]

Personally, I'm a retreat junkie. I crave them. When my daughter was born, I stopped attending retreats for a few years because I didn't want to leave her for extended periods of time. When she turned five, I went to my first retreat since I was pregnant. And I'll tell you, when I walked through the door of the retreat center, I started to cry, because I felt like I had returned home. Yes, to a place I love, but also to the part of me that is deeply at home in retreat, the place where I grow and learn and heal and dream and vision, a place where I can make myself whole.

47 ❧ DON'T DO IT ALONE

Another foundation for your personal meditation practice is a supportive group or community. This could be a group of people who meet regularly to meditate together. It may be centered on a facilitating teacher or be peer led. It could be well established or something people newly create on their own. In addition to meditating together, your community can also discuss practice issues, listen to lectures, and gather for outside activities such as potlucks.

It's a supportive experience to go to a meditation group and meditate with others. We can meet other like-minded individuals and avoid practicing in isolation—feeling like we are the only one we know who meditates. Meditating with others often provides stamina and inspiration for your practice; it's highly unlikely you will stop and check your email in the middle of a group sitting. Additionally, people describe experiencing deeper (more connected and concentrated) meditations in what I call a *group field*: a palpable energy that arises when we meditate in a group.

I realize that finding a meditation community may be easier said than done. Some of us have meditation centers or groups in our local area. If you have a teacher you are working with, there may be a community that has sprouted up around this teacher. For example, I've been leading a weekly mindfulness group since 2010 at the Hammer Museum in Los Angeles. People show up week after week to meditate in a spacious pink auditorium with two hundred or so fellow practitioners.

When you are looking for a meditation group, it's likely you may find one that practices in the Buddhist tradition, since the roots of classical mindfulness are in Buddhism. However, many religious traditions have contemplative prayer groups. And these days, you can find opportunities to meditate and study with others who are not connected to a religious tradition but solely teach classical mindfulness. Meanwhile, the Internet has actually become a repository of meditation teachings and teachers. So it's a place to look if you don't have teachers or groups nearby.

It takes just one other person to create a community. Let's say you attend a meditation retreat and connect with someone who lives far away. These days distance is really no issue. You can discuss your practice, share questions, and explore how to implement natural awareness practices in daily life all by phone, video chat, or text.

In my years of meditating, one of the supports I have come to value the most are my practice buddies. These are people I've met on retreats or in classes and who truly know me. They have a depth of understanding, and I can rely on them when I'm confused in my practice or about anything else. I contact them when I simply want to reach out and share what's going on in life. From Hawaii to San Francisco, from New York to right down the street from me, these are the people who keep me on track and connect me to my deepest love of practice.

48 ❧ FIND TWO TEACHERS

When you start a meditation practice, it is very helpful to find a teacher. Your first teacher would ideally be an accomplished meditation instructor; however, you may receive their teachings—through an online platform, from an app, or from a book, as many of us do. Finding clear guidance is key to getting started. And as your practice evolves and becomes more nuanced and deeper, it is definitely very helpful to find someone who can provide personalized guidance.

Finding a teacher isn't always easy. Going on meditation retreats or joining a teacher-led community are ways to find a teacher with whom you can discuss your practice. Some teachers are more available than others. Some take on students; some don't. You are very lucky if there are people in your area with whom you can practice and receive guidance, but many of us don't have that luxury.

A good teacher is one who has significant personal meditation experience and understands the terrain. A qualified, trained meditation teacher can offer instructions, provide tools, answer questions, and suggest how to work with whatever arises in your meditation practice. A natural awareness teacher, because they have direct experience and teach from natural awareness, can help students access natural awareness specifically. So this is Teacher No. 1: an actual person you can work with.

As we meditate over years and decades, our capacity to be our own best teacher begins to grow. This is Teacher No. 2.

Your inner teacher is a part of you that can assess your practice with a clear eye. This part of you helps you decide what type of practice to do at any given time. It can recognize when you've gotten off track and either put you back on track or help you get the right resources or support you need. Your inner teacher learns from mistakes, likes to experiment and see the results, and then makes decisions that come from the experience.

Most importantly, you, as your own teacher, have cultivated the ability to be loving and compassionate toward yourself. You have learned to teach yourself from a place of caring and passion for your practice, not from a sense of unworthiness or a problem that needs to be fixed.

Over the years, I have watched students access their inner teachers, and it's a special moment when that happens, a kind of ripening and maturation of their practice, which we can celebrate.

The two teachers are not mutually exclusive, by the way; we need them both.

A QUOTE

Once you are settled in meditation, or at any time in the day, drop this quote into a receptive mind and notice the effects. You might repeat it several times during one meditation session.

Your own consciousness shining, void,
inseparable from the great Body of Radiance,
is subject to neither birth nor death,
but is the same as the immutable Light.

ALDOUS HUXLEY[1]

PART III

EMBODIMENT

49 ❧ FORMAL AND INFORMAL PRACTICE

From time to time I meet people who experience natural awareness and then proclaim, "Great, I've got it! There's nothing more to do." Please don't go down that route. The cultivation of natural awareness takes ongoing, regular practice, both formal and informal.

Deliberately meditating is formal practice. Practicing in the midst of life is informal practice. Both types of practice mutually support each other. It is the combination of daily formal practice and daily informal practice that leads to the embodiment of natural awareness.

Formal Practice

Setting aside time to practice meditation, such as a planned and timed session in the morning or before bed (or whenever), is called our *formal practice*. A regular (and hopefully) daily formal practice will allow your natural awareness meditation to deepen, mature, and sustain. Through daily formal practice, you will gain proficiency and comfort with natural awareness meditation. It will help you to access the many gifts of natural awareness, such as contentment, joy, perspective, and insight.

Formal practice not only cultivates your ability to meditate with natural awareness but is also key to accessing and sustaining natural awareness in life. The more skilled we become in meditating with natural awareness, the more natural awareness becomes a familiar companion who shows up regularly in life. Daily formal practice is like a thread that connects us to natural awareness all throughout the day.

Additionally, formal meditation practice will give you tools to face whatever life throws at you; you will get more skilled at handling your emotions, navigating various states of mind, learning to let go, and working with physical challenges. Plus in and of itself, a daily formal meditation practice is interesting and nourishing.

So commit to your regular meditation practice, which will become the bottom line for your day. Most importantly, just do it. Practice daily, to the best of your abilities. It's okay if you miss days here and there. When you skip a day, just recommit and start again the next day.

As of this writing I have been meditating for twenty-nine years. I have certainly gone through my cycles with meditation. There have been times in my life when I was meditating two hours or more a day. There have been years when I meditated on long retreats, practicing eighteen hours a day for months at a time. There have been other times when my meditation practice has been relatively minimal or even nonexistent for periods of time. When my daughter was born, well, meditation practice turned topsy-turvy. I had to figure out how to jam it into the in-between times in my life. I discovered that the hours when she woke up to nurse at night and I couldn't go back to sleep were an excellent time to practice. Or anytime I was nursing, day or night. As she got older, my regular daily practice started to come back online, but it took a few years. However, I was able to sustain my daily informal practice (see the next section) through my daughter's early years, doing my best to practice being aware no matter what the circumstances. These days I formally meditate about a half hour daily.

Life is unpredictable, as we know. Some of us face challenges that make it hard to practice regularly, such as when we're going through a really hard time and practicing feels too painful. At other times we are on fire, and practice feels effortless and exciting. I've seen that, regardless of whether we've fallen off the wagon or are meticulously consistent, we can keep alive the flame of practice. We hold the knowledge of the power of this practice. When we see for ourselves how beneficial our daily formal meditation practice is and how it helps us embody awareness in life, we protect this flame, keeping it burning no matter how tiny it gets.

Informal Practice

Once you've established your formal practice, you can then develop an *informal practice* so that your luminous natural awareness can permeate your life. In informal practice, you bring natural awareness into your day outside of your regular formal meditation sessions.

The rest of the chapters in part III explore techniques for bringing natural awareness into our lives informally. We'll see how whispers of natural awareness can show up in the midst of life, such as when we're in nature, being creative, playing sports, or just doing nothing. We'll see how to use the glimpse practices in daily life. We'll then learn specific informal daily life practices that we can implement throughout our day.

50 ❧ DO NOTHING
THERE GOES THE BARGE

My friend Daniel's father, Dave, passed away a few years ago. Although he lived to be a few days short of ninety, I swear he looked like he was seventy. He had lived in Newport Beach, California, since the 1950s, and at noon every day—and I mean every day—he would ride his bike from his graphic design studio to the 34th Street beach and go bodysurfing.

Even after he retired, bodysurfing was his central daily activity. He had a group of friends who would bodysurf together and then spend the rest of their time just hanging out, chatting, and commenting on the surf. Daniel and I called it the Geezers' Surf Club. Dave was the elder of the group, and the younger generations on the beach admired him as a living legend.

One day about a year before his death, I visited him and Daniel. We biked down to the beach and bodysurfed. I needed a bit of coaxing, as I hate cold water (Daniel continues to tease me to this day about what a wimp I am), but eventually I did it. Bodysurfing was joyful and exhilarating for me, albeit freezing. Then we sat down on the shore. The Geezers joined us. They exchanged some stories but mostly sat in a relaxed silence.

That summer they were dredging the bay. Every afternoon at about two o'clock, a barge would motor out of Newport Harbor and chug its way north along the beach to dump its load of sand. Dave was fascinated by this barge. He was transfixed as it moved excruciatingly slowly from one end of the beach to the other, falling or rising in the water depending on whether it was carrying sand or had just dumped the sand off. Every now and then he'd announce, "Here comes the barge" or "There goes the barge."

I was perplexed. "Daniel, your dad is just watching the barge. He thinks it's amazing."

"I know," he said. "Shhhh."

That's when it dawned on me how infrequently people of my generation just sit there, like Dave was doing. There's always so much doing to be done, so little time to just be. I imagine in previous eras people used to sit on their porches, rock in their rocking chairs, and shoot the breeze, basically doing nothing. But now we can always occupy ourselves with our phones or computers, or access to the news, or crossing off items on our to-do lists.

Dave was my natural awareness guru. I decided to join him and watch the barge. And so I did. And not much happened. The barge fell and rose, and sand filled in another area on the beach. But my body relaxed, and so did my mind. I began to be suffused with a simple kind of joy that was not about getting anything—the simple joy of just being.

We can find all sorts of opportunities to just be and do nothing. Sit down somewhere and don't do anything. I mean it. Stop and put your phone away. Lie down on the grass in a park or in your yard. Soak up the sun. Drink a cup of tea and let that be all you do. Find a chair on a porch somewhere and rock. Lie in a hammock.

Are these full-on natural awareness practices? No, but they are useful practices that counteract our relentless tendencies to do and achieve and succeed and acquire. And they can foster whispers of natural awareness. It's actually an amazing practice to take twenty minutes and do nothing at all. Don't even meditate. Sit and watch a barge. It's worth it.

51 \ HANG OUT WITH CHILDREN

The other day my eight-year-old daughter and I were playing hide-and-seek. She's pretty easy to find because she always bursts into giggles anytime I'm in her vicinity. I'm a little tougher to locate and have a bit more impulse control.

In one of our bedrooms was a very bulky down comforter. I correctly surmised that if I hid under it she wouldn't notice me. So I flattened myself out the best way I could and then waited patiently. She passed by me and walked into the nearby bathroom. "Mommy, where are you?" I had done it! I was hidden. She missed me entirely. But then the attempt to keep my body flat, not move, and still breathe under the heavy down comforter seemed impossible and hilarious, and just as she reversed back into the room again, a huge belly laugh erupted from me. Naturally, she jumped on top of me. "Found you, Mommy! Why did you laugh? You gave yourself away!" And in that moment, there were she and I and the pleasure of pure being. We were together, separate, joyful, and connected, and nothing was amiss.

These little moments happen all the time. Are they full-on natural awareness? Not really—it's more like they offer whispers or glimmers of it. But we can learn to treasure these peeks at it and let them be fuel for our natural awareness practice.

Children, especially young ones, seem to me to live in a kind of timeless place. Without fail, when we are trying to get them out the door to an appointment, they have to kiss every stuffed animal they own. It frustrates us, but there is a gift in the dawdling. Children are right in the moment—present, awake. Can we meet them there? Can we put aside our adult concerns and just for a moment join their natural awareness? For some of us, it's actually quite easy, because we don't have to work at it; we can connect, enjoy, be spontaneous, let go of our agenda, and relax our mind into whichever little being is in front of us.

And by the way, you were like that too! Yup, you were little once. You dawdled, dwelled in a kind of timelessness, and experienced the wonder and amazement of life. Sometimes I think natural awareness is an invitation back to how we used to be, with the addition of wisdom, experience, and a developed prefrontal cortex.

FAKE IT TILL IT'S REAL

Sometimes natural awareness seems miles away. So just for this moment, let's pretend it's here. Right now, give it a try. You are naturally aware. You are not separate from natural awareness. Imagine it's right here.

You can repeat the phrase "It's already here" or "I'm already aware" and notice what happens. Once you try to look for natural awareness, what do you find? Rest in the way things are. Can you trust whatever is here (even if it's not *exactly* here)?

52 ❧ FIND THE FLOW IN SPORTS OR ART

Mihaly Csikszentmihalyi researched and then popularized the notion of *flow*, the idea that we can be so immersed in an activity that our sense of time stops and we are in a kind of timeless, nondistracted place. Being in a state of flow provides a feeling of well-being and mastery and often joy.

Athletes talk about this flow all the time. But you don't have to be an athlete to access it; anyone can find it in physical activity. It's also often accessed in creative pursuits, like playing music, making art, or writing. A piano player, for instance, might lose herself in her music, and it may seem like everything disappears except the playing. Others experience it when they are making love or when they are out in nature.

I'm a Zumba fanatic. The blend of Latin, hip-hop, world beat, and Bollywood dance in an entirely noncompetitive and low-key atmosphere is a blast for me. It doesn't even feel like exercise! I'm not that great at dancing—really, I'm an amateur—but I truly love it. And when I'm in the middle of a Zumba class, it feels like time stops. My connection with my body seems to make thoughts slide away into the background. I can even notice when thoughts about something not happening at the moment pop back in (*I have to remember to buy baking soda. Oh no, I keep forgetting*). That's when my sense of self reemerges and sabotages me in my happy place.

If you are an athlete or a creative person, it's likely you have experienced flow many, many times. But you might not link it to natural awareness. My hope would be that the next time you experience flow, you are able to recognize the overlap with natural awareness—that the doing has stopped and the being has begun. I wouldn't call a flow state a natural awareness state because there is likely not the component of awareness of awareness present; we are immersed in flow, but not necessarily aware that we are aware in the midst of that immersion. But if we learn to recognize these flow states, we can begin to discover moments throughout the day when we are automatically, intimately linked with our own natural awareness.

53 ◾ TAP INTO NATURE

Every year, I lecture to thousands of people about classical mindfulness meditation and natural awareness. In an introductory session, I will typically ask the audience, "Who of you has been in nature and felt connected, peaceful, at ease, and present?" Without fail, the majority of people will raise their hands.

What is it about nature that is so rejuvenating? Some of the scientific research being done about the effect of nature on our bodies and minds may illuminate the reasons. Studies out of Japan show that leisurely forest walks decrease cortisol levels, decrease blood pressure and heart rates, and reduce anxiety.[1] Some Finnish studies show that people receive emotional boosts after spending five hours a month in nature.[2]

It is my conjecture that nature somehow allows us to tap into our own natural awareness. I can speculate that it does so because it takes us back to a preindustrial state, or that the inherent beauty of nature relaxes our mind, or that nature that is untouched (or minimally touched) by human activity has a kind of freedom associated with it. Regardless of how it works, nature does seem to offer us easy access to natural awareness.

I am lucky enough to live only a short car ride away from the beach, and the other day I went walking there. At first I was lost in my thoughts, but after some time, something began to grow still inside me. Natural awareness spontaneously emerged. I didn't do much; I let the thinking play itself out until I found my mind resting, alert, aware, present, radiant, and at ease.

Everything became increasingly amusing. I felt a palpable sense of connection to all the bathers on the beach—the woman with an elaborate tattoo in the center of her back, the children rushing out to the water on their mini–boogie boards. I felt deeply content.

Then I walked too close to the water, and a giant wave breached and soaked me. And at the moment, I thought it was hilarious. I didn't freak out; I didn't think it was a problem. It was just another manifestation of life. Later I got caught up in a slow cascade of worries about work; the natural awareness began to fade, and my habitual mind took over. But being able to touch my natural awareness while being outside in nature was a nourishing break in a busy day.

I encourage you to spend alone time in nature. I know it's not possible for everyone, but even a park can positively impact your quality of being. Let your mind relax out there; let go of the worries of the day. Then see if you can tap into the connection with natural awareness that nature can foster.

Do you have cats or dogs or other creatures? Take the opportunity to just be with them. No agenda. Tune in to their quality of being, as animals exist in a space that is natural time. They may not have wisdom (I know, Lassie fans will disagree), and I can assume they don't have a sense of being aware of awareness or being able to access the natural awareness I've been pointing to through this book, but they do exist in that timeless place. No dog I know of has a to-do list.

My pet-loving students tell me that being with their animals is an easy way to access natural awareness. They speak of communing with horses or sitting for hours while petting cats or dogs. I hear story after story of a deep peace that comes over people while they are relaxing with their Persian on their lap or brushing their schnoodle. Somehow these experiences are entry points to a place of just being. What these students are experiencing is more likely a glimpse or a whisper of natural awareness than fully formed access, but how wonderful!

Why can a date with a Dalmatian put our mind at ease or take us home to resting in our radiant natural awareness? I'm speculating here (although scientific research supports the healing and therapeutic effects of pets), but perhaps being with an animal may affect us the same way that being in nature does. Just as nature can evoke natural awareness states, as discussed in the previous chapter, animals, as part of nature, can do the trick too. Perhaps it the release of oxytocin we experience when petting them that makes us feel connected in their presence. Perhaps it's that somehow their basic internal contentment seeps into us. Perhaps it is the fact that they always seem to be only in the present moment.

Whatever it is that makes being around animals such a powerful experience, it works. So try a little pet practice. Get Rover to take you into your own depth of being.

INVOKE IT

When your mind feels distracted, exhausted, lost, or disconnected, you can easily become discouraged. You might think, *How can I possibly abide in natural awareness?*

But this is when a very simple and intuitive practice becomes available to you. You can ask for natural awareness—invoke it.

Put your intention out to the world: *May I access my own innate capacity for natural awareness. May I rest in natural awareness. May I let go.* Find your own words.

You're probably thinking, *Whom am I addressing this intention to?* That's up to you to decide. Perhaps you're just addressing yourself. Regardless, setting an intention can be very powerful and opens us up to the possibility of more freedom. It's like we align with something greater than ourselves, asking the small self inside us to remember our bigger self and the innate awareness that is already present within us.

But don't trust me on this one; give it a try yourself and see what happens. Right now, pause, take a breath, and ask for natural awareness.

55 ❧ EXTEND THE WHISPERS

If you are meditating when you have a whisper of natural awareness, you can marinate in it or practice natural awareness meditation as described in chapter 21. However, when you encounter a whisper of natural awareness in daily life, then what?

Sometimes there is a sense of accomplishment—"I did it! Great, here I am. Okay, cool. Now what?" Then we grow bored or distracted or completely forget about it.

In some sense, being on the lookout for whispers is enough. Usually when we have a whisper of well-being of any sort, we skip over it. We tend to think, *Oh, that's nice*, and then we're off to whatever is next (*That was sweet, but gotta get my latte*). I encourage you not to skip the whisper, but to actually pause and enjoy it, allowing it to extend. Experience the whisper and acknowledge to yourself that you've had a taste of something meaningful. Stop and feel it. Let your body settle and drink it in a bit, rather than skipping over it, even if only for a short time. It's a bit of mini-marinating. Can you recognize the feelings in your body and mind—peacefulness, contentment, awe, openness, ease, or something else? The more we can recognize, discriminate, and acknowledge these types of whispers, the stronger they will grow and the more they will become an integral part of life on an ongoing basis.

Yesterday I was on my way to my office at UCLA, somewhat preoccupied with a call I had to make later that day. I walked from my car to the Semel Institute for Neuroscience and

Human Behavior, where my office is located. The vibrant coral trees were just starting to bloom their nearly fluorescent red display. Somehow they caught my eye, and that moment astonished me. I could have continued walking, but I remembered not to rush past life and that tapping into nature, especially in an urban environment, can reconnect me to myself. So I paused, softened my body, and took in the magnificent sight. In that moment of taking in their beauty I felt a whisper of natural awareness. I let myself rest there for a few seconds, maybe longer. My consciousness felt wide open, a warmth came into my heart, and I smiled. I stood in front of one tree for maybe a minute, basking in this sense of ease and well-being. I let the whisper expand and extend. Shortly afterward, I headed inside the building, my cell phone rang, and the connection to natural awareness seemed to dissipate. But the memory, and what I think of as the fragrance of the natural awareness, stayed with me, even when I got caught up in the busyness of the day.

56 \ BRING GLIMPSE PRACTICES INTO DAILY LIFE

Many of my natural awareness teachers use the phrase "short glimpses, many times." It helps us to see that we don't have to create special circumstances to experience natural awareness. It reminds us that uncovering natural awareness takes only a second or two and does not have to be a long, drawn-out affair.

The force of our ordinary, habitual mind is very powerful. It's constantly obscuring our capacity to experience natural awareness. Our mind is infatuated with its own drama. But we can retrain it, starting with an intention and then continuing with practices that give us glimpses or whispers of natural awareness.

All of the glimpse practices scattered throughout the book can be implemented at any moment. When we introduce them in the midst of meditation, they can be quite helpful, pointing our mind toward natural awareness. Oftentimes we can then marinate in and refresh our natural awareness meditation. But in the midst of the day, their function is truly to give us glimpses—to enable us to pause for just a second or a minute or two, maybe longer, and in that pause come home to a deeper place of well-being in the midst of life.

Pick a glimpse practice and commit to practicing it for one day or at a certain time each day for a few days. The commitment is important because if we get too laissez-faire about practicing, well, sometimes the whole day passes without much awareness.

Be sure to change up your glimpse practices too. As I mentioned earlier, glimpse practices can get kind of stale with repeated use, and they can stop "working," even if they have been working for a while. So make a point of trying new ones—even ones that haven't worked for you previously—on a regular basis. You can always come back and use your favorites again later.

Think of how an image on a computer screen is composed of dots per inch (dpi). Each dot, in and of itself, is just a tiny portion of an image, but when the dots are all connected, they make a full picture. In the same way, one little glimpse of natural awareness for a short period of time may not seem like much, but when you experience more glimpses, and they start to sustain for longer periods, they enable us to experience a fuller picture of natural awareness. Maybe you find yourself resting in natural awareness for five seconds or so once in the day. Then maybe a few times a day. Then for longer periods than just a few seconds. Later, over time, natural awareness may be available to you for several hours in the day, until ultimately you find natural awareness to be the basis for functioning.

57 ❧ GIVE YOURSELF PRACTICAL REMINDERS

Sometimes we just need to be reminded of our own capacity for being. It's easy to get caught in the stuff of life—bill paying, child rearing, relationship maintaining, and working, working, working—and we all but forget that there is something more to life than just checking things off our to-do list. As the old saying goes, we have become human doings, not human beings.

A simple solution is use whatever you have at hand to remind you. Here are some ideas that my students and I have used over the years.

Find a piece of artwork that induces peace or contentment and hang it in a prominent place in your home. I have a beautiful landscape by a local artist on the wall in front of my bed, and I sometimes meditate with it when I wake up and am too lazy to get out of bed. Just glancing at it brings a whisper of peace to my mind.

Write out a quote that is meaningful to you and place it where you will see it daily. Write quotes or reminders on sticky notes and post them around your home. How about this note: "Drop the stories and let your mind rest." Or: "Natural awareness is always here for you." Or use quotes from the glimpse practices in this book. Please be creative.

You can put a reminder on the home screen of your smartphone—maybe an image that helps you feel more wakeful or some words of wisdom. For that matter, you can train yourself to take a breath every time the phone rings, not picking it up until after you've had a moment's pause.

People often install a bell-ringing app on their computer to remind them to be present and to connect to their natural awareness. When the bell goes off hourly (or whenever), they take a mindful breath, do a quick glimpse practice, or just remind themselves that natural awareness is always available to them—whatever seems accessible in the moment.

Some people put ribbons on their wrist or wear meaningful jewelry so that each time they look down at their hands, they are reminded of natural awareness.

None of these reminders or prompts have to be complicated. The point is that it's easy for our minds to be distracted, so any kind of reminder is going to be helpful. What's most important is that you find what works for you.

The one challenge is usually that these reminders work for a while, and then our mind gets habituated to them and stops noticing them. So it's useful to change them up frequently.

I'M REMINDING YOU RIGHT NOW

We can get so caught up in our story, in our dramas, emotions, worries, and concerns—often for days, weeks, months, years—that we lose track of ourselves. So here is a reminder that can help you shift into natural awareness. Read the words slowly and let them sink in. Settle with them.

Your mind is luminous, aware, present, and radiant.

It is vast, open, and spacious.

There is nothing you have to do except shift into this recognition.

Try it now.

Shift. Relax your body. Relax your mind. Just be.

Rest in awareness.

58 \ POSTMEDITATION

Most people complete their formal daily meditation session and then get up and go straight into activity. For some of us, it can't be helped. As I've shared, my daughter waking up is usually my signal to end my meditation session, and immediately afterward, I often have to get her ready for school, without passing go or collecting two hundred dollars.

But the transition from meditation into normal activity can be an interesting and valuable part of our practice. We can notice our ordinary, habitual mind taking over. *Meditation done. Check!* And off we go.

What is the difference between the moment before and the moment after our meditation session ends? Think about it. You're right: there is no difference. The only difference is the context.

Cultivating the postmeditation state is a key to transitioning from formal meditation to informal daily life practice. Next time you finish your formal meditation session, pause for a moment. Don't get up right away. Keep the awareness sustained. If your eyes are closed, slowly open them and continue to be aware. As you stand up and walk to the coffeemaker, let whatever type of meditative awareness is present pervade. And keep going with it until you get hijacked by ordinary mind, which inevitably happens for most people.

Keep trying this way of sustaining awareness postmeditation on a daily basis and see what happens. It can be very illuminating. Sometimes the postmeditation state can last for an extended period of time. Some students have reported it lasting several hours or throughout the whole day. So attend closely to this postmeditation state, because it's an opportunity you don't want to miss.

59 ◆ WAITING? DEFAULT TO AWARENESS

I was standing in line at the Department of Motor Vehicles the other day, and I was reminded of the scene from the animated film *Zootopia* that showed a DMV run by sloths. That fictional scene seemed to be playing out right before my eyes in real life.

I had to spend hours waiting to get my driver's license renewed. Even though we've engineered as many waiting periods as possible out of our lives, there are still times when we end up waiting. Waiting is boring. It's annoying. It's a hassle. It wastes precious time. Waiting is even excruciating at times. Luckily, we always have our trusty smartphones. If you have to wait for even a moment, you can always check the weather, sports scores, Facebook, your email, the news.

One of my students informed me the other day that he had experienced a breakthrough in his natural awareness practice. He said, "When I'm waiting, or in a spare moment, I no longer default to my phone. I default to awareness." He meant that in those spaces—the ones we typically fill up with social media, texting, and Candy Crush—he practices accessing natural awareness.

So when you find yourself having to wait for something, rather than growing increasingly frustrated, rather than allowing your attention to get sucked into your devices, I'm going to echo my student and suggest another option: default to natural awareness practice.

There you are, standing in line. First notice the irritation, if it's there. Really sense in your body what the aversion feels like. Then remind yourself there are other ways with which to respond than frustration. Next, let your attention come to rest on your feet. Feel the weight of your body on the ground. Notice any obvious body sensations; take a few breaths. As you begin to pull yourself out of the aversion and into the present moment, let your awareness relax a bit.

Just staying with the sensations in your feet or body would be a fine practice. But if you want to try it, see if you can then gently open to the possibility of resting in natural awareness, right there, in the middle of the DMV—or while waiting to pick up your child, or on the phone with customer service, or at the bank. Try any of the glimpse practices: drop in a quote, attend to your back body, recall another time you've experienced natural awareness. Let your mind gently rest in the natural awareness you uncover.

Waiting is truly one of the best opportunities to do any type of awareness practice. So when you're waiting, default to natural awareness practice and see what happens.

60 ❧ TAKE A NEIGHBORHOOD WALK

One of my favorite informal natural awareness practices is taking a walk in my neighborhood.

As I head out my front door, I let my mind think—let it do its thing, whatever that may be (planning, reviewing, replaying, and so on). Sometimes I'm thinking through a thorny issue, trying to solve a problem that's been gnawing at me. But usually my mind is just reviewing the stuff of the day, like staffing issues at work or whether my daughter is watching too much TV or why I let her watch any TV whatsoever. So I let my mind ruminate, not trying to be particularly aware. I just give myself total permission to think.

After some time, my mind usually begins to calm down, and natural awareness starts to show itself, just like the sun poking through a cloudy sky for a moment or two. Again, I don't try too hard, but when I find myself glimpsing natural awareness, I acknowledge the glimpse and let it be there. Then I might fall back into thinking.

Often my thoughts turn to my surroundings: *Wow, I love what my neighbor did with her yard* or *Really? What was that neighbor thinking with that addition?* But at this point, the natural awareness is infusing the thinking. I am thinking (and sometimes even in a somewhat petty way, as I cannot help but assess architecture and landscape), but at the same time, *I am noticing the thinking occurring.* The noticing seems to be happening on its own, and I am aware of it.

Thinking slowly grows more transparent. I use this word, *transparent*, to signify the way in which thoughts seem to be part of it all. There are sights and sounds and my body in motion, and there are my thoughts and feelings and opinions (typically about design), and it is as though I can see through all of it—as if everything were transparent. Nothing appears to have weight. Everything flies by with no central sense of me.

I do go in and out of more identification with objects (my thoughts, emotions, the things around me), but often I can easily settle back into the feel of my body in motion, the sensation of my feet on the sidewalk, or the touch of the air against my skin, as well as the pleasant feeling that is in my being. The happiness of natural awareness is present for me, without my trying too hard. My mind is naturally aware, and I'm just along for the ride.

ASK YOURSELF . . .

Here's a question to ask yourself to help you access natural awareness during meditation. Once you have been meditating for a while, drop the following question into your mind. Listen deeply and see what emerges.

"Who's meditating?"

61 ◗ SHIFT (INTO NATURAL AWARENESS) WHILE DRIVING

The interesting thing about driving is that it can help us access natural awareness.

Now, if you're like most people, that's hardly how it appears.

We get into our cars, often feeling rushed and anxious. We turn on the radio to avoid being alone with our thoughts, and we smolder over what we hear about the latest human rights injustice. When a phone call comes in, we take it (hands free, of course) while shoving a granola bar into our mouths and willing ourselves not to shout at the jerk in front of us who cuts us off. Natural awareness while driving? Are you kidding? This is a more realistic driving scenario.

However, let's look at the way attention works when we're driving. In order to drive, our awareness has to be both flexible and focused. But it's actually more flexible. We open our attention quite naturally to take in an array of sensory information, including what's in our mirrors, the road in front of us, the cars behind us and to the sides, plus our hands on the wheel and feet on the pedals. An experienced driver is aware of all of these details quite naturally, without thinking about it. We actually can't be too focused when we're driving. If we were to hone in on, let's say, the license plate of the car in front of us, we would likely crash.

If this is the case, then why aren't all people driving in a flexible awareness meditative state? The main answer is that most people are lost in thought while they're driving.

Once we recognize the way flexible awareness is easily present when we drive, shifting into natural awareness while driving doesn't take much work, because so many of the elements supporting natural awareness are already there. All it takes is a shift into *awareness of awareness*: recognizing that you are aware as you're driving, that awareness is happening quite naturally. Or you can even bring in a (quick and nondistracting) glimpse practice, such as dropping in a reminder phrase or quote, to help you shift.

When I drive from natural awareness, I connect with my relaxed and aware state, noticing the road in front of me and all that my body instinctively knows how to do. I settle back, soften my belly, and let awareness be there, without trying too hard. When I notice my mind getting caught in worries ("I'm late!") and frustrations ("Stay in your lane!"), I can practice melting back into natural awareness. I still stay alert and drive well (and obviously I don't close my eyes).

One thing that is quite helpful to me is not to hold the steering wheel in the way I habitually hold it, at the clock-referenced positions of ten and two o'clock. Instead I switch to the currently recommended position of eight and four o'clock (or nine and three). This shift from my habitual way of doing things signals to my mind it's time to shift into natural awareness, and driving becomes a delight.

62 ❧ WASH YOUR DISHES
WITH NATURAL AWARENESS

Many people are familiar with an excellent instruction in classical mindfulness practice of turning an everyday activity into a mindful activity. Suggestions for such informal mindfulness practice include brushing your teeth or showering with focused or flexible awareness, for example, or remembering to be mindful each time you open your car door.

But how can we bring *natural awareness* into a routine daily activity? Certainly, repeated practice can develop a habit, thereby making natural awareness more available to us throughout the day.

Years ago, when I first started meditating, I waitressed at a Japanese restaurant. I hoped to practice mindfulness in daily life as much as possible, but I was getting discouraged at work. The restaurant was so loud and chaotic that I found it hard to focus. So I made a decision: every time I pushed on the swinging door between the kitchen and the dining area, I would be mindful. I practiced noticing the feel of my hand against the wooden door as I pressed on it.

I must have noticed my hand fifty-plus times in the course of each night, and after a while, an interesting thing began to happen. The short moments of focused awareness began to bleed into the rest of the night, and soon I found myself aware in a much less focused, more global way. I could be aware simultaneously of the sounds and the sights around me, and my balancing sushi tray, and my body, and the customers, and my coworkers. I began to relax into what seemed to be a natural awareness, without exactly knowing that was what I was doing.

My experience in the restaurant can help us think about how to bring natural awareness into daily life. Let's look at a complex activity like washing the dishes. For me, washing the dinner dishes could also include watching my daughter demonstrate her latest invented dance, a rush of table clearing, and, well, whatever chaos is happening around me as I *try* to wash the dishes. Focused awareness on, say, the feel of my hands on a dish (while it could be a great place to start) may be too restricting, especially if my awareness is being drawn to so many things.

So instead of having a single focus, I open my attention in a broad way. I wash, and I notice what it is I notice, where my attention is drawn. I relax, unclenching my belly, softening my body, and I feel an expansive sense of awareness with the full experience. Sometimes I'm watching the incredible show of me washing the dishes and watching the dance routine. I notice thoughts coming and going, sometimes capturing me, and then I practice melting back into this global sense of natural awareness. I'm often quite content, even though the story I tell myself is that I don't particularly like to wash the dishes.

Perhaps natural awareness practice is the perfect practice for parents, since with kids, there's always a certain amount of chaos and complexity going on around us. But any busy human can benefit from it.

It is also possible that natural awareness might be more suitable than classical mindfulness for complex activities, although both are valuable. Any kind of awareness is good awareness in my book!

63 ◖ WHAT TO DO WHEN YOU'RE NOT AWARE

Much of the time, we go about our day lost in ordinary mind. We think and plan and make lists and daydream and strategize and worry and obsess and laugh and talk a lot and ruminate and forget where we put our cell phones and try to call our cell phones and find that we've muted them, so we beg our daughters to search for our cell phones, and with a giggle she points to it lying on the table four feet in front of us. Our minds may or may not be suffering or particularly obsessed or problematic, but most of us are not usually resting in awareness throughout the day or even thinking about it.

Believe it or not, *we can train ourselves to be present in the midst of our inability to be present* and in doing so plant the seeds of natural awareness. The next time you recognize you're experiencing something other than natural awareness, try any one of these options.

Implement a glimpse practice on the spot. Once we recognize we're not aware, we can implement a glimpse practice on the spot. Sometimes that can do wonders. I'm waiting in line to get a bagel. The thought pops in, *Am I aware right now?* Nope. I'm a little overwrought—I'm kinda dying for that bagel. *Stop, Diana. Settle, take a breath. Remember that phrase: "Mind is like the sky with thoughts like clouds floating by." Just rest your attention right now. Got it. Ah!* Does it matter how long a glimpse lasts? Nope. Short glimpses, many times. Even a few seconds can be relieving and joyful.

Remember the shifts. You can remind yourself to practice—right in that moment—any of the natural awareness mental shifts we have talked about throughout this book: relaxing effort, broadening attention, or dropping the objects of focus. These shifts are not only meant to be implemented in formal meditation practice. They are excellent tools to use in the midst of everyday life. *Okay, I'm clearly going to wait forever for that bagel. Well, what if I were to relax my mind? Soften. Easy does it. Let me open my attention. Well, I can visually take in the whole shop, and the customers, and the smell of freshly baked bagels. And I can expand my sense of space, sight, and sound. I'm now more tuned in to the openness in the room. Hmmm, I think I'll be okay.*

Investigate the opposite. What happens when the glimpse practices or mental shifts don't work? Or let's just say the clinging is so strong that gentle reminders and mental shifts won't do much good. (*No, I really want that bagel!*) That's when we can investigate the opposite: *A relaxed, natural awareness isn't present right now, so what is? Well, I'm a little antsy. My stomach is clenched. I feel like I want to jump around. And I'm annoyed at the person in front of me who's taking forever. Why do they need four different kinds of cream cheese? Hmmm, judging is here. What does that feel like in my body? More tightness. Wow, my body is so tight—all over this one little bagel. Wow, interesting how I'm caught here! How fascinating that my mind doesn't want to let go. Can I be okay with not being okay? I guess I can.*

On a side note, in formal practice we can prepare ourselves to connect with natural awareness informally in daily life. During our formal meditation session, we can set an intention to rest in natural awareness throughout the day. (Use whatever words are useful to you.) Setting the intention to rest in natural awareness doesn't mean we will necessarily do it; it means we're holding this as a goal, and the act of setting the intention can lead to more and more awareness down the road.

Setting an intention to bring more awareness, of any type, into our lives is like plowing a field to get it ready for the plants of awareness to grow. It prepares us for the eventual flowering of our natural awareness.

WHAT'S HERE INSTEAD?

When a natural awareness isn't present, what is? See what you can find when you investigate. You may think natural awareness is not here, but is that true? What actually is here?

"What's here" may be a mood, an emotion, bodily sensations, particular thoughts, sights, sounds, or anything at all. So it's helpful, when you realize that you're feeling far away from accessing natural awareness, to ask yourself the question "What's here instead?"

Can you notice an emotion moving through you like a weather pattern? Can you feel the changing physical sensations, your body alive in every moment? Sometimes in the process of investigating what's here we notice the transparency of whatever we take to be real and present. Suddenly, more natural awareness may present itself to you. As you investigate what's here instead, you might ask, "Who is aware? What is knowing that 'this' is here?"

64 ❧ PRACTICE WHILE YOU LISTEN

Since the 1990s, my colleague Marvin G. Belzer has taught classical mindfulness practices to college students, originally at a state university. These students, from all over the Midwest and from a variety of backgrounds, found meditating to be a life-transforming experience.

There were always a number of students who enjoyed the classes yet hated to meditate. They'd fidget in class, spacing out during the meditations. Still, they wanted to be there. When Marvin introduced relational mindfulness practices—done in pairs, triads, or groups—something changed. He offered opportunities for them to speak and listen to each other in a structured way that gently invoked mindfulness. Students then began to report how they finally "got" mindfulness for the first time.

My experience is that when I teach people relational mindfulness practices, students often begin to tap into, not just mindful listening, but also natural awareness. In other words, they move from trying to listen to someone (making an effort) to a simple natural awareness (being effortlessly present with another human being).

Here are some basic guidelines for mindful listening and speaking: When you are the listener, give your full attention to the other person. If your mind wanders, bring it back, and notice your body from time to time to stay centered. When you are speaking, speak authentically about what's true for you.

Slow down and also notice your body from time to time. Verbalize what you're aware of in the moment, if you wish.

These might seem to be a lot of guidelines at first. But students say that once they get the basics down, they drop the guidelines and simply show up. They can offer their full presence to another, not interrupting, not trying to fix them, not judging or having to do anything special. The listener often reports feeling like they are being truly heard for the first time.

From my view, there is also typically a kind of settling in to natural awareness without much effort on the part of either party.

You can explore this relational mindfulness practice at home, either formally (recruit a friend, and each of you takes two minutes to talk while practicing the guidelines) or informally (just try to be present with another whenever it makes sense to do so). Natural awareness may be accessible in a simple and consistent way merely by opening to it during our everyday interactions with others. And when people complain they don't have enough time in the day to meditate, I usually say, "Well, how much time do you spend talking?" Tap into natural awareness in every conversation. Don't leave home without it!

65 ❧ PRACTICE IN COMPUTER HELL

Here's another example of how we might practice all kinds of awareness in daily life when we really need it.

I have a seven-year-old laptop computer. It's definitely on its way out. I sat down to write this morning, and it started acting funny—fading in and out of programs in a weird way. I'm used to its peculiar behavior; I usually just restart it. I had, however, recently installed a new operating system, and I wasn't exactly clear if it was too much for my ancient computer. So I restarted it and sat there and waited. And waited. And waited. It was one of the slowest restarts I've ever experienced.

I realized I might as well take the opportunity to practice awareness. I was, after all, writing a book on natural awareness. I was sitting outside, so I broadened my attention to take in the sights and sounds around me. I watched the play of light, tuned in to the vast blue sky. That was relaxing . . . for a minute or two. Then I noticed impatience. Okay, forget flexible awareness. I shifted to a more focused awareness: *What am I feeling in my body? Impatience, pretty intensely. Contraction in my belly. Okay, can I just be with this?* As I felt the contraction for a minute, it actually relaxed, and I once again opened to the scene around me. I watched the leaves moving in the breeze, which touched me, and I tried a glimpse practice of using words to evoke natural awareness: *Relax your mind, Diana. Let everything be unaltered, exactly as it is.* I could feel my internal contractions loosen even more.

Sitting there in natural awareness for a few minutes, I heard a voice that was *definitely* not a cloud in the sky say, *Wow, this is taking a really long time. Do you think something is wrong?* My mind started to worry, and rather than that thought dissolving into the sky of my mind, it picked up steam. *What if my computer has finally blown a gasket? This thing has been running on fumes. Okay, breathe, just come back to your breath*—a classical mindfulness reminder.

I'm too impatient! shouted my inner voice. I got up. I couldn't take it. I wanted to distract myself. So, honestly, I did. I watered two plants. But then I walked mindfully for a minute or two, focusing on the feel of my feet on the ground, and a thought appeared: *You don't know what's going to happen. And whatever it is, you can handle it.*

As I heard these words, a soft feeling of ease came over me again. Then another thought, in a kind of whisper: *And it doesn't actually matter. You'll figure it out.* I had melted back into natural awareness.

And then, as a sign of mercy, the screen shifted, and my desktop popped up. Except all my files were missing. *What the heck happened?* (Boy, was I caught!) *What if my book has been erased?! Maybe I installed a virus! Those hackers can do everything these days. Aaaah*—panic!

Okay, Diana, just feel the panic. I breathed into the agonizing feeling in my belly (classical mindfulness). *Worst-case scenario, you can call your editor and tell her what happened, and she can extend the deadline. And you do have a backup. (Yeah, but from twelve days ago!) Calm down. Breathe.* I started to gain some mindfulness and calm.

And then that spinning rainbow beach ball from hell showed up on my computer screen. How I hate that thing! But I know from experience that spinning beach ball icons on Macs are an excellent time to simply let go and be. So I just did that. Feeling my body, but trying also to rest my mind, looking, listening, softening. I felt tears of frustration and let them be there.

Finally, everything popped up, and there it was—my book on my computer, totally back to normal. And in the moment, the story dropped away, and life was okay again. My mind settled, and I felt some gratitude for my meditation practice. I set about writing again.

But first I backed up the entire book into my Dropbox account and then ordered the new computer that I had been putting off for a year.

66 ❧ AN ETHICAL LIFE

Earlier we covered the idea that just because you can rest your mind in natural awareness and have experienced subtle or profound connection to states of well-being, it definitely doesn't mean it's time to kick back and do whatever you want.

I know the experience of resting in natural awareness can feel like "It's all good" or "Wow, there's something timeless that I have tapped into. I got it!" These are wonderful feelings, but they don't mean now life is a free-for-all. "Since we're all connected, I'll just borrow your car and not give it back." We have to behave ethically, or this deep understanding is simply conceptual.

Padmasambhava, a famous Tibetan Buddhist historical figure and natural awareness master, was reputed to have said, "Though my view is as spacious as the sky, my actions and respect for cause and effect are as fine as grains of flour."

We can think of ethical behavior as based on respect and nonharming—living a life where we uphold basic common-sense morality that includes not killing, not stealing, not lying, and being wise about our consumption and our sexuality. These ethical guidelines are present in most religious traditions and are the foundations of secular ethics as well. And they are key to awareness practices.

When I *live in integrity*—sticking to these basic ethical guidelines and living as closely aligned as possible with my best self—my meditation practice is significantly improved. To put it simply, I don't spend my entire meditation session stressing out or feeling guilty about something I did.

I learned this lesson the hard way when I lived in the Buddhist monastery. About four months into my meditation retreat, I was possessed by vivid, nonstop memories of stealing doll clothes from another child when I was about ten. Not merely a few dresses, but about fifty of them, over many months. During the retreat, my mind kept reliving this incident from twenty years earlier, and the replay lasted a full week. I could not get the memory out of my head, nor could I escape the accompanying shame and guilt that circulated in my consciousness, until finally the replay played itself out. Eventually I had to forgive myself (I mean, I was ten, after all).

Our behavior impacts our mental state. When we live in an ethical way, we see the results in our meditation practice. When we are not tormented by thoughts of ways we wish we hadn't behaved, we likely can have a clearer and more concentrated mind.

Then it becomes a cycle: As our mind gets clearer and more stable, and as we gain more insight into ourselves through our classical mindfulness and natural awareness practices, we stop wanting to act in unethical ways. We see the benefit of acting and living in integrity. We also live with more of a sense of connection to all of life, and that promotes kind and ethical behavior because we see we're not that separate from anyone else or this planet. Hurting you is like hurting me.

Living in integrity can bring us inner joy. It doesn't stop with us. Our families and communities benefit from us modeling and living with integrity. And when we blow it—and of course we do—we find ways to make amends, quickly and sincerely, and recommit to a life of integrity.

AN OCEAN ANALOGY

Read this analogy slowly and let the image sink in—not to dwell on it, but to see how it impacts your consciousness.

Imagine your mind is like the ocean. On the surface of the ocean are choppy waves and turbulence. This is the drama we get caught in: thoughts, fears, emotions, and stories. Now, an ocean may have a choppy surface, but imagine sinking below the surface into the infinite depth below. Deep in an ocean is a boundless stillness that is completely undisturbed by the turbulence above. Can you connect with this deep tranquility?

67 ❧ SOMETHING CHANGES INSIDE

Some of us have small glimpses of natural awareness that permeate our meditation practice or even our day. Others may have a more dramatic experience, such as an event we identify as "waking up." This awakening may have occurred recently or long ago, in meditation practice or in daily life. Some students recall clearly seeing into themselves in a way that created a foundational shift in their being.

When a big shift occurs, often we think, *Great! I'm going to be like this forever! I'll always feel expansive, connected, loving, and joyful.*

Well, the feeling may last, and sometimes it lasts for a while. For the truly lucky, it utterly transforms us forever. But for the rest of us, usually we go back to being more or less the same—still crabby in the morning, anxious about our teenager, enraged by the lousy driver ahead of us. Sometimes we wonder about that experience and think, *Did it really happen? Life seems so ordinary; I'm still the same.*

We are human. In many ways, we still are the same after our experience. But bigger experiences of natural awareness can result in a profound internal shift that does change us—just not always in the way we expect.

The first change we might experience is that we can frequently recall these natural awareness experiences, and when we create conditions for their arising (going on retreat, committing to a daily meditation practice), they come back to us.

We start to realize that shifting our mind into a relaxed and receptive state is possible whenever we remember and create the space for it to arise. Natural awareness may be momentarily obscured, but it is always available to us.

Second, when we connect to this state, something inside us that is beyond our cognitive understanding is transformed. Our mind may try to process the experience and make sense of it. We may attempt to categorize it, mentally checking off a list the ways in which our perspective has shifted or what positive qualities we may have attained, but I have seen, in myself and my students, that the change goes much deeper than that.

Something has shifted deep inside, and, well, you can't really go back. It's hard to explain or put a finger on. Maybe we're a little less reactive, a little quicker to smile, a little less likely to blame. We're living our realization without actually having to do much. It's altered us, somehow.

But we do have to keep practicing, or this change goes dormant. And continuing, lifelong practice is what keeps our meditation vibrant and interesting.

68 \ WHAT WILL YOU LET GO OF?

In the last chapter, I described the internal changes that often happen after we have a profound experience with natural awareness. At the same time, because there has been a deep shift within us, we may have to look at our lives differently. Perhaps before our changes, we viewed reality in terms of what we could attain or whom we could use to further our goals. After our changes we may find that world view getting turned on its head. We often recognize that the fundamental truths underlying human existence are compassion and connection. And then we may have to ask ourselves big questions like "How do we live now? How can we live our life in alignment with our deepest understandings?"

We might ask, for instance, "Whom am I spending my time with, and how are they contributing to my sense of well-being?" I've given up toxic friendships in which I've felt the other person was constantly critical of me. Many students report having to let go of unsupportive relationships and actively working to create friendships with others who are aligned with them in values and equally on a spiritual quest.

Other big questions we may find ourselves asking include:

- Am I doing work that is meaningful? Is my work aligned with my integrity and the understanding that has come though my practice?

- How am I spending my time? Are Facebook and bad reality TV the best food to feed my consciousness? What can I do with myself in my free time that reflects and nurtures my deepest values?

- How am I feeding my body? What am I ingesting—junk food and sodas, or food that is nourishing and healthy?

Underlying all of these questions is *the* big question: "What will I let go of? What may I have to sacrifice in order live a life aligned with my values and my deepest understandings?" The answer may be not so easy, but the question is an important one. "What am I willing to sacrifice?"

My experience is that as we practice and live connected to our understandings, and as we commit to our spiritual journey, the answers to all of these questions slowly become clear. We find ourselves naturally letting go of things that no longer serve us. Sometimes it's incredibly painful, but when it's in the service of living in alignment, well, we're willing to feel the pain, because it's the pain of deep, healthy growth.

What are you willing to let go of?

69 ❧ AND IT'S OKAY

Guess what? Even after we do years of natural awareness practice, despite glimpses big and small, despite even feeling significantly transformed at some point, we're still us. So when we do go back to our habitual ways of being following some kind of transformational experience—when we yell at our eight-year-old because she exploded a bowl of yellow-food-coloring-infused milk all over the kitchen and it took two hours to clean the entire mess (but who is bitter?)—it's actually okay.

When we go on a meditation retreat and have beautiful glimpses or hours of peace and deep abiding in our own natural awareness, and then we sit down to meditate a week later, and all we can do is scratch our mosquito bites and worry about an upcoming deadline at work—it's okay.

And when our concentration practice makes us feel like our mind could ignite a piece of newspaper, and then we turn to natural awareness and feel dull and hopeless and bored—it's okay.

And when you read parts of this book and they make no sense whatsoever, and you just go back to whatever meditation you were doing before—it's okay.

Please don't assume you will always live in natural awareness and life will be bliss. We are human. And guess what? Being human is a pretty cool thing.

Ordinary life is lovely, when we show up for it. Even watering our plants or rolling over in bed are sublime moments of being human. Sometimes during the day I pause whatever mundane activity I'm doing and announce to myself: "Diana, this is your life." I remember a Kurt Vonnegut essay in which he talked about standing in line at the post office, chatting people up, purchasing a stamp, and at the end he said, "We are here on Earth to fart around. Don't let anybody tell you any different."[1]

Some students relentlessly beat themselves up when they lose touch with natural awareness or when their meditation practice is shot and they return to habitual mind states. Do me a favor: please don't do that. Natural awareness is an extraordinary state of being that with gentle, relaxed persistence can become more and more who we are. But if we judge ourselves for our return to ordinary mind, we're really missing the point. Let's keep it simple: We can be aware or identified, free or caught. And when we're free, it's pretty wonderful. And when we're not, it's okay. Just take a breath, relax, and do your best to let go.

You can do it. It's okay. It's okay. It's okay.

A QUOTE

Pause, settle, and drop this quote into your receptive mind and notice the effects. You might repeat it several times during one meditation session or at any moment of the day.

> Only one thing made him happy
> and now that it was gone
> everything made him happy.
> LEONARD COHEN[1]

70 🔖 I CAN HANDLE IT!

When my daughter was young, she was very sensitive to loud noises and crowds. So I made an effort to keep her away from situations that might cause overwhelm.

However, she loved fairies, and one day when she was four, we learned that a nearby preschool was hosting a fairy play for Halloween. I asked her if she wanted to go and warned her it might be noisy and crowded. She carefully weighed the noise versus the fairies, and the fairies won out. So we decided to risk it.

The school was decorated with twinkle lights, colorful silk scarves, and shiny cutout paper stars and flowers. There were adult staff members and parents in fairy costumes and probably fifty preschoolers also dressed in costumes (many of which were not fairylike but more of the Spider-Man and princess variety) and running around like little hyperactive gerbils, barely able to contain their excitement.

There was noise—lots of it.

When we arrived, immediately I could feel my body tense. I knew this was not going to go well. My daughter hated this kind of thing. So my first response was to downplay. I put on a fake smile. "Well, look at this! It's not too crowded. It's really not that noisy."

My daughter had my number. "Mommy, you're wrong. It *is* noisy." She paused and then added, "But I can handle it."

I was blown away. She did fine. And she knew she would be fine. Though she clung to me at times and we left a little early,

212

she enjoyed the play, and I believe she reveled in her coura-
geous act. And just in case you're wondering, although she still
has some noise sensitivities, she did outgrow them. She has, in
recent years, enjoyed baseball games (go, Dodgers!) and even
more than survived the crowds of a Tokyo train station.

I tell this story because it captures a key aspect of both natural awareness and classical mindfulness practices: They give us
a capacity to handle life. Despite the ups and downs of these
practices, despite challenges, students often reflect that their
mind is more at ease, more balanced, and they are able to face
whatever life brings—even our everyday versions of the noisy
fairy play.

71 ◆ FINDING A NEW ADDRESS

I've noticed that many students live in states of fear, grief, depression, and anger. They take up permanent residence on Anxiety Street. Or they've moved all their furniture onto Depression Avenue, and it sure feels like home. Or perhaps it's Self-Judgment Lane, and . . . well, you get the picture.

Because of years of habit and conditioning, perhaps because of childhood trauma or other adverse experiences, and because we have not been taught anything different, our inner sense of normalcy (or "home," as I'm calling it) has been associated with our neuroses.

Let's take an example: For those of us who live on Comparison Boulevard, it can feel like the entire world is conspiring to show us that we are inadequate. Everything proves it. Your friend gets a promotion, and rather than feel joy for them, your mind habitually reverts to grief, comparison, and replaying the failure feeling because you didn't get a promotion too.

Sadly, these kinds of responses are utterly normal for many people's minds. We are so used to feeling anxious, for instance, that it becomes our address, the place where our mind defaults to or lives all the time.

It's normal! So normal that when we feel something different— like, for instance, peace—we simply don't know what to do with it.

I've had many students over the years come to me and say, "Um, since I've been meditating, I've started having this

214

feeling, and I don't know how to describe it. It comes for a few seconds, and it's, well, it's kind of . . . um . . . peaceful."

"Hurrah," I say. "Yes! You've had peace." These students are so unfamiliar with peace and related states that they barely can recognize them. Others have described that the self-critical, anxious, or depressed chatter in their head, which they've had for as long as they can remember, has gradually lessened, and they don't even know who they are. It's as if they are now a different person—or have moved to a new address. In my view, they are starting to live connected to natural awareness.

I recommend moving, if possible, to Peaceful Street, or Equanimity Lane, or Joy Avenue. I guarantee these are better mental neighborhoods than where most people live most of their lives. This is not to deny challenging emotions or the ups and downs of life, but to point out that there are healthier places for our minds to reside. And when we live on Natural Awareness Boulevard, we have the capacity to handle whatever life brings because our baseline is not neurosis, but luminous awareness.

72 ❧ YOU CAN LIVE FROM NATURAL AWARENESS

Over time, as students increasingly encounter natural awareness in meditation and in daily life, they begin to function from it.

This is completely doable. *You* can do this.

Students report that they may not be living in some exalted state all the time, but the deep letting-go experience of natural awareness is just a shift of their mind away. When they are caught in challenging emotions, they remember to settle back, let go, and meet the difficulties with awareness. They find themselves frequently "melting back" or "dropping the banana." This becomes second nature.

Many say that over time they take the ups and downs of life much less personally. When difficulties or challenges arise, they are affected, but their minds tend to move more quickly toward letting go, toward more relaxation and ease. Once a mind has had deep tastes of this kind of freedom, it knows it wants to keep returning there.

Other students report a sense of inhabiting their lives more fully. Many of us feel like we have been on autopilot or entirely checked out for a lifetime. With more awareness, life can appear as if it goes from black and white to Technicolor! With practice, we experience life more fully—have deeper connections, more gratitude for even the smallest things—because we are present to it. One student of mine reported, "Oh wow, this is my life! I finally get it!"

Well-being becomes a baseline for people. An internal sense of safety, contentment, and ease becomes a kind of default way of being rather than a special or unusual moment. It doesn't mean that life is always good for them; that is hardly the case. What it does mean is that at our core, we have cultivated a capacity to handle all that life brings, and we live with this confidence and in deep relaxation. *We know that we can't control life, but we can control how we relate to our experiences, no matter what they are.*

As people transform, they continue to practice. They grow their daily meditation practice, they bring natural awareness into daily life, they use the glimpse practices whenever they remember, and they attend retreats for intensive practice periods. And after a time, natural awareness becomes second nature. They begin to function from natural awareness instead of functioning from ordinary mind. Sometimes there are days when natural awareness seems to be the dominant mode in their being. Other times it is only subtly available. Sometimes natural awareness feels distant, even for long periods of time. Other times it is a constant companion.

The bottom line is that with meditation and daily life practices, any of us can uncover and abide in our luminous natural awareness. We can find freedom right in the midst of life. We can open our heart to great compassion and wisdom, and we can live in joy and profound contentment each and every day. And you can do it, too.

ASK YOURSELF . . .

Here's a question to ask yourself to help access natural awareness. Pause and settle, then drop the following question into your mind. Listen deeply and see what emerges.

"Who would you be if you were fully you?"

AFTERWORD
EVOLUTIONARY IMPERATIVE

As I sit in my living room reading the Sunday newspaper, I am inundated with stories and images of tragedies, violence, greed, impending environmental catastrophe, and despair. Sometimes I say to myself, in light of the horrors of these days, "Why am I writing a book telling people to meditate? Shouldn't we be out on the streets?"

Well, these actions are not mutually exclusive, and from time to time I am out on the streets. But what I've come to see is that natural awareness practice, and any other meditation practice, has profound effects on individuals, which in turn impacts families, professional lives, neighborhoods, and institutions of which we all are a part.

When we live connected to our natural awareness, we have an ongoing experiential sense of well-being that can counteract the depression and anxiety that paralyze so many of us. Since many of us struggle with these symptoms, a healthier planet can begin with healthier individuals, and meditation is a proven mental-health strategy.

Individual transformation is the beginning. By engaging natural awareness, many of us have an experiential sense of connectedness, and from this comes compassion. What causes separation—greed, violence and hatred, the creation of the "other"? As we practice, we move from the theoretical to the embodied sense that we are connected; we come to know intuitively that doing harm to another is like harming ourselves or our loved ones. How do we bridge religious, cultural, political, and social divisions? We begin with the willingness to listen, to not hold so tightly to our views, and to truly be in the presence of another without an agenda.

I have seen meditators leave unfulfilling jobs in sectors that were exploitative to live a life of service. I have taught activists how to meditate and seen their resultant activism be infused with equanimity, power, and compassion rather than routine anxiety, powerless rage, and despair. I have known meditators who bring principles of awareness into conflict resolution on the global level. I have observed meditators make compassionate choices in the face of horrific odds—not because kindness makes a nice theory, but because their inner understanding tells them this is the only way to act.

So rather than being navel-gazing, which meditation is occasionally accused of, it is absolutely connected to outer change. I believe that for human survival, there is an evolutionary imperative for all of us to wake up—to wake up to our inner suffering and learn how to reduce it, and then wake up to the suffering of others and of the planet. We need to act from a mind that has reduced its clinging, that defaults to awareness and compassion, that lives from a place of connectedness. When these realizations are second nature, there is no question in my mind that each individual will contribute to the cultural and institutional change that is so deeply needed in this time. It is urgent that we practice—and let this practice mature—so that we can become agents of peace.

NOTES

Introduction

1. In recent years, the word *Vipassana* has become associated primarily with the teachings of S.N. Goenka and his worldwide network of Vipassana meditation centers. However, Vipassana is actually a general word meaning "insight" or "seeing clearly." A wide range of Vipassana meditation techniques, originating in Southeast Asian Buddhist countries, are currently being taught in the West. They are variably called Vipassana, insight, or mindfulness meditation. My teachers studied under Mahasi Sayadaw, whose lineage is different from Goenka's.

Part I. Foundations: Understanding Natural Awareness

Chapter 1. What Is Natural Awareness?

1. Wikipedia, s.v. "awareness," last modified April 15, 2018, 23:56, en.wikipedia.org/wiki/Awareness.

Chapter 9. The Science of Natural Awareness Practice

1. Dominique P. Lippelt, Bernard Hommel, and Lorenza S. Colzato, "Focused Attention, Open Monitoring, and Loving Kindness Meditation: Effects on Attention, Conflict Monitoring and Creativity—A Review," *Frontiers in Psychology* 5 (2014): 1083, doi.org/10.3389/fpsyg.2014.01083.

Glimpse Practice: A Quote (Between chapters 11 and 12)

1. Dudjom Lingpa, *Heart of the Great Perfection: Dudjom Lingpa's Visions of the Great Perfection*, trans. B. Allan Wallace (Somerville, MA: Wisdom Publications, 2016), xv.

Part II. Techniques: Meditating with Natural Awareness

Chapter 17. Classical Mindfulness Meditation: Focused Awareness Practice

1. Although listening to sounds is technically a flexible awareness practice (see chapter 19), since our attention is not staying fixed on one object but moves around from sound to sound, listening to sounds can serve as a helpful anchor for many people. In this case, our anchor is a group of objects, not a single object. Because it can calm and stabilize our mind, I include it in the beginning meditation instructions. Alternatively, some people focus on the changing body sensations they feel (such as the sensations in their hands or feet) as their anchor.

Chapter 20. Shift into Natural Awareness

1. For more information on the Wheel of Awareness, see: Daniel J. Siegel, *Aware: The Science and Practice of Presence—The Groundbreaking Meditation Practice* (New York: Tarcher Perigee, 2018).

Chapter 21. Natural Awareness Meditation: Marinate and Refresh

1. Loch Kelly, *Shift into Freedom: The Science and Practice of Open-Hearted Awareness* (Boulder, CO: Sounds True, 2015), 28.

Chapter 35. Embodiment: Don't Get Caught in the Head

1. James Joyce, "A Painful Case," in *Dubliners* (London, 1914; Project Gutenberg, 2001), gutenberg.org/files/2814/2814-h/2814-h.htm.

Chapter 46. Retreats

1. I teach at Spirit Rock Meditation Center in Marin County, California. It is a wonderful retreat center, and I encourage you to visit its website spiritrock.org.
2. Dan Harris, *10% Happier: How I Tamed the Voice in My Head, Reduced Stress Without Losing My Edge, and Found Self-Help That Actually Works—A True Story* (New York: Dey Street Books, 2014), 121.

Glimpse Practice: A Quote (Between chapters 48 and 49)

1. Aldous Huxley, *Island* (New York: Harper Perennial, 2009), 318.

Part III. Embodiment: Living Natural Awareness

Chapter 53. Tap into Nature

1. Florence Williams, *The Nature Fix* (New York: W.W. Norton, 2017), 23.
2. Williams, *The Nature Fix*, 139.

Chapter 69. And It's Okay

1. Kurt Vonnegut, *A Man Without a Country* (New York: Random House, 2007), 62.

Glimpse Practice: A Quote (Between chapters 69 and 70)

1. Leonard Cohen, *Only One Thing*, 2007, pigment print, 15 × 12", Drabinsky Gallery, Toronto. Reproduced in Robert Enright, "Leonard Cohen," *Border Crossings* (December 2007), bordercrossingsmag.com/article/leonard-cohen.

APPENDIX

GUIDED MEDITATION ON THE SPECTRUM OF AWARENESS PRACTICES

In this meditation we will practice three different types of awareness on the spectrum of awareness practices, moving from focused awareness to flexible awareness to natural awareness. You can have someone read it to you as a guided meditation, or you can read it aloud yourself on a recording device and then listen to it. Or you can simply read it in print to see how you might practice across the spectrum.

 As you find a comfortable posture, closing your eyes if you wish, notice how you're doing in this moment. Be curious about your body and mind. Take some breaths. Try to maintain an attitude of kindness, of settling into your own sense of being. It's right here for you, in every moment—this human capacity to be aware.

Starting with **focused awareness**, bring your attention to your meditation anchor—that which you always return to. If your anchor is your breath, receive your breath in your abdomen, chest, or nose, feeling the sensations of breathing—rising, falling, expansion or contraction, coolness or tingling. One breath ends, and the next breath begins.

Or your anchor can be sounds. You can listen to the sounds come and go around you. Listen to them without getting lost in stories about the sounds. No need to analyze or reject a sound; just listen. When your attention wanders, you can notice it, mentally say the word *thinking* or *wandering*, and then return your attention to your anchor.

Keep returning every time you notice yourself lost in thought. Let all other objects (thoughts, emotions, sensations) stay in the background; focus on your anchor, return when you get distracted. Continue in this way for a few minutes.

(*Period of silence.*)

Now, when a new object (such as emotions or sensation) becomes very obvious, calling out to you, let go of your anchor and turn your attention to whatever this new object is. Feel the emotion or sensation in your body. Notice what happens to it as you pay attention to it. Stay with this new aspect of experience until it no longer holds your attention, until it stops, or until something else grabs your attention. Can you notice the changing nature of the object that pulls you away?

Ultimately, return to your anchor, to your breath or the listening. Your attention has become more flexible.

(*Period of silence.*)

If you want to explore a fully **flexible awareness**, you can try it now. Sensations, sounds, thoughts, and emotions may be coming and going in the background. Let go of your meditation anchor and turn your attention to these background objects. Settle back and notice whatever is obvious to you as it arises and passes. No need to return to your anchor.

There's a sensation; it increases. A sound pulls you, then a memory. You feel your heart racing, and you take a breath. And there's a sensation in your foot, and so on. Emotion arises, a sound grabs you. These are examples, but you can notice what pulls your attention. It might be very subtle; it might be more obvious. Just follow what is most obvious in your experience.

(*Period of silence.*)

As you transition into **natural awareness**, I invite you to relax your body and mind. Rest. No need to try too hard. We are naturally aware. Your mind is aware without you doing anything. Can you sense and feel this awareness that's present right here, all the time? Our minds are luminous, bright, and radiant like the sun. Can you sense that?

Rest. Nothing to do. Let go of having to make any effort.

Open your senses. Listen to the sounds around you. Let your hearing capacity extend as far as you can imagine.

Now feel the back of your body on the chair or cushion, in space. Unclench your belly and expand the awareness of space around your body. Move outward 360 degrees—back, front, up, down.

If you wish to open your eyes, you can expand your visual field. Keep your eyes soft, seeing out peripherally. Notice if it's possible to hear, sense, and see in this expanded way.

Can you feel your inner experience simultaneously embodied? Can you be external and internal at the same time? Your mind is open, spacious, and limitless, like the sky. Your thoughts are like clouds floating by, temporarily obscuring the sky-like nature of your mind. Marinate here for a while.

If you start to feel contracted or confused, you always have the present moment to return to. You always have your breath, your body. Then, when you feel like it, relax into a more spacious knowing. You can notice thoughts dissolving into the vast field of awareness.

Marinate in natural awareness for as long as you are drawn to. Whenever you feel ready, you can conclude your meditation session.

ABOUT THE UCLA MINDFUL AWARENESS RESEARCH CENTER

The Mindful Awareness Research Center (MARC) at the University of California, Los Angeles (UCLA), is located in the Semel Institute for Neuroscience and Human Behavior in the UCLA medical school. The mission is to foster mindful awareness across the lifespan through education and research in order to promote well-being and a more compassionate society. MARC faculty members, in collaboration with the UCLA Cousins Center for Psychoneuroimmunology, research mindfulness interventions, and the teaching staff offer a rich variety of mindfulness classes for the university community, for the Los Angeles community, and beyond through online programming. MARC is a pioneer in mindfulness teacher training, with its Training in Mindfulness Facilitation. For more information, including many free guided and downloadable meditations, go to marc.ucla.edu.

ACKNOWLEDGMENTS

This book is a product of so many influences, starting with my students at the UCLA Mindful Awareness Research Center, from whom I learn all the time, and my teaching colleagues through MARC, Spirit Rock Meditation Center, and students all over the world.

I am indebted to my teachers and feel so lucky to have received their incredible teachings for nearly thirty years. I would not be sharing this today if it were not for Venerable Sayadaw U Pandita of Burma, who built my meditation foundation with precision, utter clarity, and a crotchety but compassionate heart.

I have had the great fortune to study and practice with a range of masters who teach different versions of the natural awareness practices, including the Tibetan Dzogchen, Thai Forest, and Zen traditions of Buddhism and Advaita Vedanta and other lineages of Hinduism. I have also learned much from my insight meditation teachers and colleagues who have explored and taught from this territory.

The natural awareness teachings I am sharing here have been profoundly influenced by Joseph Goldstein, Tsoknyi Rinpoche and his lineage, Charles Genoud, Sharda Rogell, Guy Armstrong, Valentino Giacomin, Jack Kornfield, Ajahns Sumedho and Amaro, Loch Kelly, Tara Brach, Donald Rothberg, Adyashanti, and *The Tibetan Book of Living and Dying*. Other important influences include Eugene Cash, Deborah Chamberlin-Taylor, Michael Craft, Joanna Macy, Marie Mannschatz, Michele McDonald, Sharon Salzberg, Maylie Scott, Alan Senauke, Thanissara, and Pamela Weiss. Leslie Keenan, Rachel Howard, and Sara Hurley have gracefully influenced the healing of so many other aspects of my life that support my inquiry into natural awareness.

This book has been significantly improved with the insightful, detailed comments of Guy Armstrong, who over the years has so effortlessly clarified the merging and differentiation of the many practice streams. I am grateful to Marvin G. Belzer, my partner in crime for just about every aspect of teaching, and his wisdom that shaped the foundations of this book; Amita Schmidt for years of friendship, support, comments on the book, and unceasing investigation into reality; Daniel Doane for barge (and other) clarifications; Annaka Harris for her careful attention to language and accessibility issues; Keith Hennessey for thoughtful answers to complex questions; Amy Berfield for her design eye; and Phillip Moffitt and Dawa Tarchin Phillips, who offered sage advice in the eleventh hour. I also want to thank James Baraz, who encouraged me to write what would give me joy.

Thank you to Melissa Valentine for inviting this book to be born; to my agent, Stephany Evans, who has given unending support and encouragement for so many years; and to my editor, Amy Rost, whose brilliant, detailed edits helped me clarify everything I wanted to say. I could have never arrived at the book you are holding in your hands without her generous encouragement and perceptive eye. And to all the staff at Sounds True who, across the board, have expressed genuine enthusiasm in this project. "Team Being" includes acquisitions editor Jennifer Brown, production editor Jade Lascelles, copyeditor Diana Rico, book interior designer Beth Skelley, and Jennifer Miles, whose cover art so beautifully captures the spirit of this book.

Much love and appreciation to the extended Winston Clan: Marvin, Iza, Nicolas, Geoff, Mona, Maia, and Matthias. And without a doubt, my biggest gratitude goes to Roni Rogers, my mother. I credit the existence of this book to her unending willingness to babysit, as well as her insightful comments to help shape it. And Mira, my love, you (and your generation's future) are the point of everything.

ABOUT THE AUTHOR

Diana Winston is the director of mindfulness education at UCLA's Mindful Awareness Research Center and the coauthor, with Susan Smalley, PhD, of *Fully Present: The Science, Art, and Practice of Mindfulness*. Called by the *Los Angeles Times* "one of the nation's best-known teachers of mindfulness," she has taught mindfulness since 1999 in a variety of settings, including hospitals, universities, corporations, nonprofits, and schools in the United States and Asia. A sought-after speaker, she developed the evidence-based Mindful Awareness Practices curriculum and the UCLA Training in Mindfulness Facilitation, which trains mindfulness teachers worldwide. She is a founding board member of the International Mindfulness Teachers Association.

Her work has been mentioned in the *New York Times*, *O, the Oprah Magazine*, *Newsweek*, the *Los Angeles Times*, *Allure*, *Women's Health*, and a variety of other magazines, books, and journals. She is also the author of *Wide Awake: A Buddhist Guide for Teens* and has published numerous articles on mindfulness.

Diana was trained as a meditation teacher by Jack Kornfield and is a member of the Spirit Rock Teachers Council at Spirit Rock Meditation Center in Northern California. She has been practicing mindfulness meditation since 1989, including a year as a Buddhist nun in Burma (now Myanmar). Currently Diana's most challenging and rewarding practice involves trying to mindfully parent an eight-year-old. For more information, please visit dianawinston.com.

ABOUT SOUNDS TRUE

Sounds True is a multimedia publisher whose mission is to inspire and support personal transformation and spiritual awakening. Founded in 1985 and located in Boulder, Colorado, we work with many of the leading spiritual teachers, thinkers, healers, and visionary artists of our time. We strive with every title to preserve the essential "living wisdom" of the author or artist. It is our goal to create products that not only provide information to a reader or listener, but that also embody the quality of a wisdom transmission.

For those seeking genuine transformation, Sounds True is your trusted partner. At SoundsTrue.com you will find a wealth of free resources to support your journey, including exclusive weekly audio interviews, free downloads, interactive learning tools, and other special savings on all our titles.

To learn more, please visit SoundsTrue.com/freegifts or call us toll-free at 800.333.9185.